INDIAN VEGETARIAN COOKBOOK

INDIAN VEGETARIAN

COOKBOOK

Tarla Dalal

St. Martin's Press

New York

Back cover shows Vegetable Ring (page 31), Bean Hotpot (page 55) and Green Peas Renedy (Page 102).

Cover and inside photography by Bob Komar, Illustrations by Sue Lines.

INDIAN VEGETARIAN COOKBOOK, Copyright 1983 The Hamlyn Publishing Group Limited. All rights reserved. Printed in Italy . No part of this book may be used or reproduced in any manner whatsoever without written permission except in the case of brief quotations embodied in critical articles or reviews. For information address St. Martin's Press, 175 Fifth Avenue, New York, N.Y. 10010.

Library of Congress Cataloging in Publication Data

Dalal, Tarla.
   Indian vegetarian cookbook.

   1. Vegetarian cookery. 2. Cookery, Indic.
I. Title.
TX837.D17 1985   641.6'5   85-1991
ISBN 0-312-41403-X

ISBN # 41403X

First published in Great Britain by The Hamlyn Publishing Group Limited.

First U.S. Edition

Contents

Useful Facts and Figures

Notes on metrication

Exact conversion from Imperial to metric measures does not usually give very convenient working quantities and so metric measures are rounded off into units of 25 grams. The table below shows the recommended equivalents.

Ounces	Approx g to nearest whole figure	Recommended conversion to nearest unit of 25	Ounces	Approx g to nearest whole figure	Recommended conversion to nearest unit of 25
1	28	25	11	312	300
2	57	50	12	340	350
3	85	75	13	368	375
4	113	100	14	396	400
5	142	150	15	425	425
6	170	175	16 (1 lb)	454	450
7	198	200	17	482	475
8	227	225	18	510	500
9	255	250	19	539	550
10	283	275	20 ($1\frac{1}{4}$ lb)	567	575

Note: When converting quantities over 20 oz first add the appropriate figures in the centre column, then adjust to the nearest unit of 25. As a general guide, 1 kg (1000 g) equals 2.2 lb or about 2 lb 3 oz. This method of conversion gives good results in nearly all cases, although in certain pastry and cake recipes a more accurate conversion is necessary to produce a balanced recipe.

Liquid measures

Imperial	Approx ml to nearest whole figure	Recommended ml	Imperial	Approx ml to nearest whole figure	Recommended ml
$\frac{1}{4}$ pint	142	150 ml	1 pint	567	600 ml
$\frac{1}{2}$ pint	283	300 ml	$1\frac{1}{2}$ pints	851	900 ml
$\frac{3}{4}$ pint	425	450 ml	$1\frac{3}{4}$ pints	992	1000 ml (1 litre)

Spoon measures All spoon measures given in this book are level unless otherwise stated.

Oven temperatures
The table below gives recommended equivalents.

	°C	°F	Gas Mark
Very cool	110	225	$\frac{1}{4}$
	120	250	$\frac{1}{2}$
Cool	140	275	1
	150	300	2
Moderate	160	325	3
	180	350	4
Moderately hot	190	375	5
	200	400	6
Hot	220	425	7
	230	450	8
Very hot	240	475	9

Notes for American and Australian users
In America the 8-oz measuring cup is used. In Australia metric measures are now used in conjunction with the standard 250-ml measuring cup. The Imperial pint, used in Britain and Australia, is 20 fl oz, while the American pint is 16 fl oz. It is important to remember that the Australian tablespoon differs from both the British and American tablespoons; the table below gives a comparison. The British standard tablespoon holds 17.7 ml, the American 14.2 ml, and the Australian 20 ml. A teaspoon holds approximately 5 ml in all three countries.

British	American	Australian
1 teaspoon	1 teaspoon	1 teaspoon
1 tablespoon	1 tablespoon	1 tablespoon
2 tablespoons	3 tablespoons	2 tablespoons
$3\frac{1}{2}$ tablespoons	4 tablespoons	3 tablespoons
4 tablespoons	5 tablespoons	$3\frac{1}{2}$ tablespoons

An Imperial/American guide to solid and liquid measures

Imperial	American	Imperial	American
Solid measures		**Liquid measures**	
1 lb butter or		$\frac{1}{4}$ pint liquid	$\frac{2}{3}$ cup liquid
margarine	2 cups	$\frac{1}{2}$ pint	$1\frac{1}{4}$ cups
1 lb flour	4 cups	$\frac{3}{4}$ pint	2 cups
1 lb granulated		1 pint	$2\frac{1}{2}$ cups
or superfine sugar	2 cups	$1\frac{1}{2}$ pints	$3\frac{3}{4}$ cups
1 lb confectioners' sugar	3 cups	2 pints	5 cups ($2\frac{1}{2}$
8 oz rice	1 cup		pints)

Introduction

In India cooking is an art and a tradition handed down from generation to generation, from mother to daughter. Until the advent of cookbooks, all cookery instruction was oral and practical and, whereas certain items like dals, flour and rice were measured, important flavoring ingredients (like spices and masalas) were added according to individual judgement. In fact, until quite recently it was not uncommon for locally published cookbooks to mention ingredients like ginger, chilies and spices without giving any exact quantities. As a result, dishes made from the same list of ingredients showed marked variations in taste from family to family and region to region. Slight variations do not always make the dishes less tasty and hopefully you will feel encouraged to experiment with the recipes in this book.

The parts of India which have a strongly vegetarian population naturally offer a wide selection of vegetarian fare, but in Bengal and coastal areas where fish is plentiful, vegetable dishes tend to be supplementary to the main diet and there are few specialities. However, the popular cuisine of the Punjabis, a vigorous and zestful people, includes both vegetarian and non-vegetarian specialities. With greater mobility people now have an increased awareness and appreciation of foods and dishes from other parts of the country. It is no surprise, therefore, that traditional family cooking is gradually being influenced and altered. The British introduced vegetable cutlets many years ago when they entertained their strictly vegetarian Indian guests and today, ingredients like bread, butter, cheese and Western seasonings such as tomato catsup are increasingly being used in Indian cooking – even methods like baking are becoming popular. Many of the recipes also reflect these new trends which are developing in Indian cooking.

Despite changes of this sort, it is perhaps the special ingredients that make Indian cooking stand out from the cuisine of other countries. Ghee, for example, is a form of clarified butter which is widely used. However, because of its high cost, ghee made from butter is gradually being replaced by hydrogenated vegetable oils which are known as 'vegetable ghee'. Groundnut and other oils are also used for cooking in many parts of India. Dahi is another common ingredient and in its place, yogurt has been specified in the recipes. Other distinctive ingredients made from milk are paneer and khoya. Although the use of spices is common throughout the Orient and coconut is used in coastal areas and islands, the manner in which spices are used in India

8

is quite distinct. The numerous combinations of spices and masalas are important for the flavor of the finished dish and the fresher the masalas the better the results. A wide variety of lentils and dals are also used – moong, toovar, urad, gram and masoor dal are just a few of the more common types.

In India, a great deal of importance is attached to food and eating, and in the past the preparation of meals has tended to be a leisurely and long drawn out affair. However, times and tastes are changing. Amongst other things time-saving methods and short cuts are now important to the Indian housewife. Bearing this in mind, all the recipes in this book are extremely easy to follow and although the ingredients list may seem a little formidable at first you will find that the following basic items will cover the spice combinations for most of the recipes – garlic, coriander seeds, cumin seeds, red chilies and and chili powder, cinnamon, cloves, black pepper, cardamom and ginger. I am sure you will find the scope for experimenting with different ingredients and spice combinations an exciting prospect and worthwhile experience. I wish you good eating and many moments of happiness.

Kitchen Equipment

In keeping with the changing times, many urban Indian kitchens now have modern conveniences like refrigerators, pressure cookers, blenders, grinders and gas ovens. In addition, traditional equipment and utensils are invariably present. Some of the traditional equipment required for the recipes is described below along with suggested modern alternatives.

For grinding purposes, the pestle and mortar are used for small quantities and a rough-surfaced, black stone grinding slab with a stone roller is used for larger quantities and pastes. Whereas hand grinding gives better results, the electric grinder or blender saves time and hard work. In either case, masalas ground just before they are to be used bring out the best flavor in any dish.

Chapatis and parathas are traditionally rolled out on a circular wooden rolling board (known as a 'patla') using a rolling pin ('velan') which is thicker in the centre than it is at the ends. The rolled-out breads are cooked on a slightly curved iron plat – a 'tava'. They are turned during cooking with the help of a long pair of metal tongs, with flat ends which give a good grip, and these are known as 'chipya'. Instead of these items, a rolling pin can be used and the breads can be cooked in a heavy-based skillet or griddle with the help of a spatula.

Deep frying is done in a 'kadhai' which is a wide-mouthed metal vessel similar to a Chinese wok. The deep-fried food is removed from the ghee or oil with the help of a slightly curved perforated ladle with a long handle – a 'jhara'. The jhara doubles up as a sieve for dropping batter into the fat for making bundis (page 116). A pan designed for deep frying can be used instead of the kadhai and a slotted spoon can be used to replace the jhara.

Traditions and Menus

Most Indians serve their meals on flat circular plates with shallow rims. These are known as 'thalis' and are made either of brass (tinned inside) or stainless steel or, for the well-to-do, of silver. The liquid foods such as dals or curries are poured into cylindrical bowls known as 'katoris' and these are arranged either on or near the thali depending on its size. In earlier times, food was served on plantain leaves or on a circular mat made by fastening dried leaves together with thin sticks like toothpicks and the liquid food was served in bowls made from dried leaves. This practice is still followed in the smaller towns and villages.

Generally speaking, all items of food such as breads, dals, curries, pickles and accompaniments such as raitas are served together, although rice and poppadums may be offered separately. Desserts are not eaten daily but when served, they are usually eaten with the meal. Savories, some of which can also be eaten as snacks, are also served with the meals although, like desserts, they are not eaten daily. No drinks are served except cold water and in some parts of India like Gujarat, salted buttermilk. Food is eaten with the fingers as knives and forks are just not appropriate for eating the Indian breads. The method of eating these is to tear off a portion of bread and use it to scoop some dal, curry or vegetable. The food is usually eaten with the right hand; and the left hand, which is kept clean, is used for drinking water and also for taking additional portions of the dishes.

The type of food and the manner of eating varies from region to region but generally speaking, a combination of a vegetable dish, curry or dal with bread and an accompaniment, followed if desired by a rice dish, would be fairly representative of a typical menu. Soups and desserts are optional. Boiled rice goes better with the spicier dals and curries. Similarly, in combining breads with curry, a good rule would be to use plain parathas, chapatis or puris with a spicy curry or dal and to serve yogurt with the spicier rotis and parathas. I have included a recipe for a sweet bread – such breads are commonly eaten at festivals in Western India. By way of guidance, I have suggested a few menus and you can follow these before making up your own combinations of dishes.

MENUS

VEGETABLE AND DAL SOUP (page 15)
MOGLAI POTATOES (page 34)
MASALA DAL (page 50)
POTATO ROTI (page 82)
CUCUMBER SALAD (page 74)
BOILED RICE (page 123)
PANEER AND COCONUT BALLS (page 114)

———————— * ————————

YOGURT SHORBA (page 14)
KHAMIRI PEA PURIS (page 83)
SPICY YOGURT (page 77)
MASALA KHICHADI WITH CURRY SAUCE (page 72)
NARANGI NI BASUNDI (page 120)

———————— * ————————

VEGETABLE AND RICE SOUP (page 15)
EGGPLANT IN CHILI-GARLIC SAUCE (page 41)
SWEET & SOUR VEGETABLES WITH
CRISPY NOODLES (page 32)
MANCHURIAN VEGETABLES (page 32)
ORANGE SANDESH (page 119)

———————— * ————————

PANEER MUTTER KORMA (page 44)
BROAD BEAN CURRY (page 54)
KORMA RICE (page 69)
MOONG DAL TIKKAS (page 106)
POPPADUMS (page 77)
MALAI PUDAS (page 117)

Soups

Soups are optional extras in Indian meals as they do not form part of traditional menus. However, many Indian ingredients can be used to enliven vegetable soups: aromatic spices, hot or mild chilies, dals and yogurt all add interest to these simple dishes.

In this chapter the soups range from a refreshing and spicy Yogurt Shorba to an unusual Vegetable Soup with Crisp Vermicelli which is served with chilies in vinegar. There are filling soups, too, like Vegetable and Dal Soup or Vegetable and Rice Soup; served with parathas these are substantial enough to form a meal on their own.

When you plan to serve soup along with other dishes, then present it as a first course with poppadums or chapatis. If the soup is to be served hot, it is important to make sure that it is steaming hot and not just lukewarm. Try to remember that the starter should tempt the appetite for the rest of the meal, so before you pour the soup into bowls taste it to make sure that the seasoning is just right and serve moderately sized portions which are not too filling.

Yogurt Shorba

Serves 4

2 cups yogurt
1 teaspoon all-purpose flour
2 tablespoons milk
2 tablespoons ghee
$\frac{1}{2}$ teaspoon cumin seeds
$\frac{1}{2}$ onion, chopped
2 green chilies, chopped

$\frac{1}{2}$ teaspoon grated fresh root ginger
salt to taste
2–4 teaspoons chopped tomatoes
2 tablespoons chopped cucumber
1 tablespoon chopped fresh
coriander leaves

1 Beat the yogurt, flour and milk together.

2 Melt the ghee and fry the cumin seeds in it for a few seconds. Add the onion, green chilies and ginger. Continue to fry for a few seconds.

3 Stir in the yogurt mixture and salt. Add the tomato and cucumber, heat until the mixture just boils, then remove from the heat. Serve immediately, sprinkled with the chopped coriander.

Lentil and Tomato Shorba

Serves 6

1 tablespoon oil or ghee
2 onions, sliced
2 cloves garlic, pressed
$1\frac{1}{4}$ cups masoor dal, washed

4 cups tomatoes, chopped
6 cups water
salt to taste
a little boiled rice to serve

1 Heat the oil or ghee in a saucepan. Add the onions and garlic and fry for 2 minutes. Add the dal and tomatoes, then continue to cook for 5–7 minutes.

2 Pour in the water and bring to the boil. Reduce the heat, cover the pan and simmer until the dal are soft. This should take about 30–40 minutes.

3 Allow the soup to cool slightly, then purée in an electric blender, and strain through a sieve. Return the soup to the saucepan. Heat through, taste and adjust the seasoning, then serve hot topped with a little boiled rice.

Vegetable and Dal Soup

Serves 4

3 large onions, chopped
4 large tomatoes, chopped
4 tablespoons moong dal
6 cups water

2 tablespoons butter or 1 tablespoon oil
1 lb cabbage, shredded
1 lb spinach, chopped
salt and pepper to taste

1 Mix two-thirds of the chopped onions and half the chopped tomatoes with the dal in a saucepan. Pour in the water.

2 Bring to the boil, cover the pan and simmer for 1 hour. Purée in an electric blender, then strain through a sieve.

3 Melt the butter or heat the oil in a saucepan, add the remaining onion and fry for 1 minute. Add the cabbage and spinach and continue to fry for 1 minute. Pour in the strained stock, bring to the boil and boil for 10 minutes.

4 Stir in the remaining chopped tomato, salt and pepper, bring to the boil, then cook for a few minutes. Serve hot with Parathas (page 80) or Potato Roti (page 82).

Vegetable and Rice Soup

Serves 4

$\frac{1}{4}$ cup butter
1 onion, chopped
1 quantity vegetable stock (page 122)
4 cups mixed vegetables

$\frac{1}{2}$ cup long-grain rice
2 cups milk
1 teaspoon lemon juice
salt and pepper to taste

1 Melt the butter in a saucepan, add the onion and cook for 1 minute. Add the stock, bring to the boil and boil the soup (uncovered) for 10 minutes.

2 Prepare the mixed vegetables according to their type and cut into bite-sized pieces. Add to the soup. Bring to the boil and cook for 20 minutes.

3 Add the rice and cook, uncovered, for a further 15 minutes. Stir in the milk, lemon juice, salt and pepper. Heat through, simmer gently for a few minutes, then serve.

Vegetable Soup with Crisp Vermicelli

Serves 6–8

3 tablespoons oil
2 cups cabbage, shredded
1 cup carrots, thinly sliced
$\frac{1}{2}$ cucumber, thinly sliced
1 tomato, sliced
a few lettuce leaves, shredded
$\frac{1}{2}$ teaspoon monosodium glutamate
6 cups vegetable stock
(page 122) or water

oil for deep frying
$\frac{1}{2}$ lb rice vermicelli, cooked
and drained
CHILIES IN VINEGAR
2 red or green chilies
2 teaspoons white vinegar
soy sauce to serve

1 Heat the 3 tablespoons oil in a saucepan. Add the prepared vegetables and monosodium glutamate. Cook for 2–3 minutes, stirring frequently.

2 Add the stock or water and bring to the boil. Cook for 2–3 minutes.

3 Heat the oil for deep frying to 350 F, add the cooked vermicelli and fry until crisp and golden. Drain on absorbent paper, crumble the crisp noodles and add them to the soup.

4 Slice the red or green chilies into rings, discarding the stalks. Mix them with the vinegar.

5 Serve the soup immediately with soy sauce and the chilies in vinegar.

Curried Vegetables in Tomato Sauce (page 23) with folded Chapatis
(page 80) and yogurt with chopped fresh coriander

Sour and Hot Pepper Soup

Serves 6–8

2 red chilies
2 teaspoons white vinegar
2 tablespoons cornstarch
$\frac{1}{4}$ teaspoon pepper
1–2 tablespoons soy sauce
6 cups vegetable stock
(page 122) or water
2 tablespoons oil

2 carrots, grated
2 cups cabbage, shredded
1 onion, sliced
2 scallions, chopped
$\frac{1}{4}$ teaspoon monosodium glutamate
salt to taste
chili garlic sauce (page 41) and soy
sauce to serve

1 Slice the red chilies into rings, discarding the stalks. Mix them with the vinegar.

2 Blend the cornstarch, pepper and soy sauce with a little of the stock or water until smooth. Add the remaining stock or water, pour into a saucepan and bring to the boil, stirring continuously.

3 Heat the oil in a skillet, add the carrots, cabbage, sliced onion, scallions and monosodium glutamate. Fry, stirring, over high heat for 3–4 minutes.

4 Add the fried vegetables to the cornstarch mixture. Stir in the chilies in vinegar and salt. Bring back to the boil and cook for a few minutes.

5 Serve immediately with chili garlic sauce and soy sauce.

Pages 20/21 *Clockwise from top left: Spiced Vegetables with Buttered Rice (page 27), Vegetable Ring (page 31), Coconut Curry Sauce (page 75) and Paneer Makhani (page 48)*

Vegetable Dishes

Vegetables, rice and dals together make up the main part of an Indian vegetarian diet. Prepared and cooked according to their type, a wide variety of vegetables is used in dishes which can be either hot or mild in flavor. Seasoned with specially selected whole or ground spices, simple vegetables are cooked in rich sauces for mouth-watering results. Alternatively, they may be chopped or mashed and molded into vegetable koftas, then deep fried until crisp and golden.

In this chapter you will find that the recipes make full use of all these different cooking methods. Layered in baked dishes, shaped into patties or simply served whole and spiced – there are as many different ways of presenting vegetables as there are types to choose from.

And, when you're in a hurry, don't forget that frozen vegetables can also play a part in many of the recipes. Quick to prepare and cook, with an excellent flavor and color, certain frozen vegetables – for example corn and peas – can be used instead of, or as well as, fresh ones.

Vegetable Curry

Serves 4

8 cups mixed vegetables — for
example, green beans, carrots, peas,
potatoes and cauliflower
2 onions, chopped
½ fresh coconut, grated
10 mild red chilies
10 teaspoons poppy seeds
7 cloves garlic
½ teaspoon turmeric

1-in piece fresh root ginger, grated
¼ cup ghee
½ teaspoon garam masala (page 124)
1¼ cups water
1 cup yogurt
3 tablespoons light cream
1 teaspoon sugar
salt to taste

1 Prepare and cook the mixed vegetables according to their type, breaking or cutting large ones into bite-sized pieces.

2 Grind the onions, coconut, chilies, poppy seeds, garlic, turmeric and ginger to a paste.

3 Melt the ghee in a heavy-based saucepan, add the paste and cook for 3–4 minutes. Stir in the garam masala and cook for a further few minutes, then add the vegetables and water. Bring to the boil and cook for a few minutes.

4 Stir in the yogurt, cream, sugar and salt, heat gently, then serve hot with parathas (page 80).

Sabzi Panchmahal

Serves 4

2 tomatoes
3 onions
1 cup water
8 cups mixed vegetables – for
example, green beans, carrots,
potatoes and peas
1 tablespoon chopped cashew nuts
1 tablespoon poppy seeds
5 cloves garlic

2 teaspoons coriander seeds
1 teaspoon cumin seeds
7 red chilies
½-in piece fresh root ginger, grated
3 green cardamoms
¼ cup ghee
salt to taste
4 tablespoons light cream
½ teaspoon sugar

1 Put the tomatoes in a bowl, pour in boiling water to cover and leave to stand for 1 minute. Drain, skin and chop.

2 Roughly chop the onions and place them in a saucepan with half the water. Bring to the boil, cover and simmer for about 15 minutes, or until the onions are soft. Purée in an electric blender.

3 Prepare the vegetables according to their type, cutting large ones into bite-sized pieces, and cook lightly in boiling water. Drain and set aside.

4 Grind the cashew nuts, poppy seeds, garlic, coriander and cumin seeds, chilies, ginger and cardamoms to make a paste.

5 Melt the ghee in a heavy-based saucepan, add the paste and cook for 2–3 minutes. Stir in the chopped tomatoes and blended onion, then cook for a further 3–4 minutes.

6 Add the vegetables, salt and remaining water to the pan. Bring to the boil and cook at a simmer for a few minutes. Stir in the cream and sugar, make sure the sauce is well mixed and serve hot.

Curried Vegetables in Tomato Sauce

(Illustrated on page 17)

Serves 2

8 cups tomatoes	1 teaspoon cumin seeds
$2\frac{1}{2}$ cups water	2 pinches asafoetida
4 potatoes	3 tablespoons gram flour
$\frac{1}{2}$ lb okra	1 cup green beans
13–14 green chilies	a few curry leaves
1-in piece fresh root ginger, grated	1 tablespoon garam masala (page 124)
$\frac{1}{4}$ cup ghee	salt to taste
1 teaspoon mustard seeds	

1 Quarter the tomatoes, place them in a saucepan and add the water. Bring to the boil, reduce the heat and simmer for 20 minutes.

2 Strain the cooked tomatoes through a sieve, or purée in a blender, then strain through a sieve. Cut the potatoes and okra into bite-sized pieces.

3 Grind ten of the chilies and ginger to make a paste. Split the remaining chilies open and reserve them for later use.

4 Melt the ghee in a heavy-based saucepan, add the mustard seeds, cumin seeds and asafoetida, then cook for a few minutes. Stir in the gram flour and cook, stirring, over gentle heat for 2–3 minutes.

5 Gradually pour in the blended tomatoes, stirring continuously. Add the prepared vegetables, green beans, curry leaves, remaining green chilies, garam masala, paste and salt.

6 Bring to the boil, reduce the heat and cover the pan. Simmer for 15–20 minutes or until the vegetables are cooked. Serve hot.

Overleaf *Clockwise from the left: Khamiri Pea Puris (page 83), Moglai Potatoes (page 34), Vegetable Rolls (page 101), tomatoes with chopped fresh coriander, cucumber with chili powder and mango chutney*

Ceylonese Curry

Serves 4

2 fresh coconuts
5 cups water
8 cups mixed vegetables – for
example, carrots, peas and green
beans
$\frac{1}{4}$ teaspoon turmeric
1$\frac{1}{2}$ teaspoons ground coriander
1$\frac{1}{2}$ teaspoons ground cumin
2 teaspoons chili powder
3 small cinnamon sticks
5 peppercorns
$\frac{1}{2}$ teaspoon ground fenugreek

2 onions, chopped
4 curry leaves
2 green chilies, slit
salt to taste
2 potatoes, boiled and finely
chopped
3 large tomatoes, finely chopped
SAMBOL
$\frac{1}{2}$ fresh coconut
1 onion, chopped
1 teaspoon chili powder
1 teaspoon lemon juice

1 Pierce two of the eyes in the top of each coconut and drain off the coconut water. Crack open the nuts, remove and grate the flesh.

2 Place the grated coconut in a bowl with 1$\frac{1}{4}$ cups of the water. Leave to stand for 30 minutes, then gradually chop the mixture in a blender and strain it through a fine sieve to obtain thick coconut milk.

3 Add the remaining water to the sieved coconut flesh and allow to stand for a further 30 minutes. Blend and strain this mixture as before to obtain thin coconut milk.

4 Meanwhile, prepare the mixed vegetables, cutting any large ones into bite-sized pieces.

5 Pour the thin coconut milk into a saucepan. Add the vegetables, turmeric, coriander, cumin, chili powder, cinnamon sticks, peppercorns, fenugreek, chopped onions, curry leaves, slit chilies and salt. Bring to the boil, reduce the heat and cook until the vegetables are tender – about 15 minutes.

6 Stir in the potatoes, tomatoes and half the thick coconut milk. Cook for a few minutes before adding the last of the thick coconut milk.

7 To make the sambol, remove and grate the flesh from the coconut. Grind the grated coconut with the remaining ingredients and salt to taste to form a paste.

8 Serve the heated curry with plain cooked rice, cooked vermicelli or thin noodles and the sambol.

Spiced Vegetables with Buttered Rice

(Illustrated on pages 20/21)

Serves 6

2 dessert apples, cored
1 red or green pepper, trimmed
1 tomato
8 cups vegetables – for
example green beans, carrots, peas
and potatoes
1 onion, chopped
4 green chilies
1-in piece fresh root ginger, grated

2 tablespoons ghee
1 teaspoon chili powder
$\frac{2}{3}$ cup tomato catsup *or*
fresh tomato purée
$\frac{2}{3}$ cup water
salt to taste
2 cups long-grain rice
$\frac{1}{4}$ cup butter
3 tablespoons light cream

1 Roughly chop the apples, pepper and tomato. Prepare and cook the mixed vegetables according to their type. Grind the onion, chilies and ginger to make a paste.

2 Melt the ghee in a saucepan, add the paste and cook for a few minutes. Add the apples, pepper, tomato and the chili powder. Cook for 3–4 minutes. Stir in the vegetables, tomato catsup or tomato purée, water and salt to taste, then cook for a few minutes, until heated through.

3 Cook the rice according to the instructions on page 123. Set aside and allow to cool. Melt the butter in a saucepan, add the rice and salt to taste. Toss to mix, then heat through over low heat.

4 Stir the cream into the spiced vegetables and serve with the buttered rice.

Spiced Vegetables

Serves 4–6

8 cups mixed vegetables – for
example green beans, carrots,
courgettes and cauliflower
2 onions, chopped
6–7 green chilies
1-in piece fresh root ginger, grated
$\frac{1}{3}$ cup ghee

3 potatoes, boiled and cubed
2 tablespoons chopped fresh
coriander leaves
$\frac{1}{2}$ teaspoon garam masala (page 124)
1 teaspoon lemon juice
salt to taste

1 Prepare and cook the vegetables according to their type. Grind half the chopped onion to a paste with the chilies and ginger.

2 Melt the ghee in a saucepan, add the remaining onion and fry for 1 minute. Add the paste and continue to fry for 1 minute.

3 Add the mixed vegetables, potatoes, coriander, garam masala, lemon juice and salt. Cook, stirring, for a few minutes to heat through. Serve hot.

Baked Masala Vegetables

Serves 4–6

1 small cauliflower, lightly cooked
4 carrots, cooked
2 onions, chopped
3 green chilies
$\frac{1}{2}$-in piece fresh root ginger, grated
oil or ghee for deep frying
12 small new potatoes
$\frac{1}{4}$ cup butter

$\frac{1}{2}$ teaspoon chili powder
1 cup peas, cooked
salt to taste
SAUCE
2 tablespoons butter
$\frac{1}{4}$ cup all-purpose flour
$2\frac{1}{2}$ cups milk

1 Cut the cauliflower into florets and cut the carrots into long strips. Grind half the chopped onion to a paste with the chilies and ginger.

2 Heat the oil or ghee for deep frying to 350 F, add the potatoes and cook until golden brown. Drain on absorbent paper and set aside.

3 Melt the butter in a saucepan and fry the remaining onion in it for a few minutes. Add the paste and fry for a further $\frac{1}{2}$ minute. Stir in the chili powder, cooked vegetables and salt to taste, then transfer the mixture to an ovenproof dish.

4 To make the sauce, melt the butter in a saucepan, stir in the flour and cook, stirring, for 1 minute. Gradually pour in the milk and bring to the boil, still stirring. Add salt to taste.

5 Pour the sauce over the vegetables and bake in a hot oven (450 F) for 20 minutes or until browned on top. Serve immediately.

Pea and Potato Patties (page 35) and Gado Gado (page 78)

28

Quick Baked Vegetables

Serves 4

4 cups mixed vegetables – for
example, green beans, cauliflower,
carrots, and peas
2 potatoes, boiled
ghee for deep frying
1 eggplant, sliced
1 lb tomatoes
1 cup water
$\frac{1}{4}$ cup butter

1 onion, chopped
1 tablespoon all-purpose flour
$\frac{1}{2}$ teaspoon chili powder
1 teaspoon chili sauce (optional)
1–2 teaspoons sugar
1 teaspoon vinegar
salt to taste
$1\frac{1}{2}$ cups paneer, chopped (page 122)
2 tablespoons light cream

1 Prepare and lightly cook the mixed vegetables according to their type. Slice the potatoes. Heat the ghee for deep frying to 350 F and cook the potatoes until lightly browned. Drain on absorbent paper. Deep fry the eggplant in the hot ghee.

2 Roughly chop the tomatoes and place them in a saucepan with the water. Cook gently for 15 minutes or until the tomatoes form a pulp. Strain through a sieve and set aside.

3 Melt half the butter in a saucepan and fry the onion for 1 minute. Add the flour and fry for a further $\frac{1}{2}$ minute. Stir in the tomato pulp, chili powder, chili sauce (if used), sugar, vinegar and salt. Mix well. Add the mixed vegetables, 1 cup of the paneer and cream, then cook for a few minutes to heat through.

4 Arrange a layer of potato and eggplant slices in an ovenproof dish. Spread the vegetable mixture over, then layer the remaining potato and eggplant slices on top. Top with the reserved paneer.

5 Dot with the remaining butter and bake in a hot oven (450 F) for about 15 minutes. Serve immediately.

Note: Grated hard cheese can be used instead of the paneer as a topping for this dish.

Vegetable Ring

(Illustrated on back cover and pages 20/21)

Serves 6

4 medium potatoes
salt to taste
4 cups mixed vegetables –
for example, green beans, carrots,
and peas
large bunch of fresh coriander
leaves, trimmed and chopped
6 green chilies
1-in piece fresh root ginger, grated
4 tablespoons grated fresh coconut
juice of 1 lemon

1 teaspoon sugar
2 cups cooked long-grain rice
2 cups frozen corn, cooked
6 tablespoons oil
2 teaspoons mustard seeds
4 teaspoons sesame seeds
4 tablespoons chopped cashew nuts
1 tomato, sliced
1 green pepper, sliced
2 pinches asafoetida

1 Peel and quarter the potatoes, place them in a saucepan and cover with water. Add a little salt, bring to the boil, then reduce the heat and cover the pan. Simmer for 20 minutes until the potatoes are tender, then drain and mash them.

2 Prepare and cook the mixed vegetables according to their type and dice any large ones.

3 Meanwhile, grind the chopped coriander leaves with the chilies, ginger, coconut, lemon juice and sugar to make a paste. Add 1 teaspoon salt to the paste.

4 Combine the potatoes, mixed vegetables, rice and corn. Add the paste, season with salt to taste and mix well.

5 Heat half the oil in a heavy-based skillet, add half the mustard seeds and fry for 1 minute. Add half the sesame seeds and half the nuts and continue to fry for a few minutes.

6 Stir the fried ingredients into the vegetable mixture.

7 Arrange the tomato and pepper slices in the bottom of a well-greased ring mold.

8 Spoon the vegetable mixture into the mold, pressing it down well. Cover with foil and bake in a moderately hot oven (400F) for about 40 minutes.

9 Heat the remaining oil in a skillet, add the remaining mustard seeds and cook for 1 minute. Add the asafoetida, the remaining sesame seeds and nuts. Fry, stirring, for a few minutes.

10 Turn out the vegetable ring on to a hot serving dish. Pour over the fried mixture and serve hot with Coconut Curry Sauce (page 75).

Sweet and Sour Vegetables with Crispy Noodles

Serves 4

small head cabbage
$\frac{1}{2}$ lb cauliflower
1 large tomato
2 carrots
1 onion
$\frac{1}{4}$ teaspoon monosodium glutamate
salt to taste
2 cups canned pineapple slices
1 lb Chinese egg noodles

SAUCE
5 tablespoons white vinegar
$\frac{2}{3}$ cup tomato catsup
2 tablespoons sugar
1 tablespoon all-purpose flour
3 tablespoons oil
oil for deep frying

1 Shred the cabbage and thinly slice the cauliflower, tomato, carrots and onion. Mix all the vegetables, add the monosodium glutamate and salt.

2 Reserve the sirup from the pineapple and chop the slices into pieces.

3 Cook the noodles in plenty of boiling water until tender – about 10 minutes. Drain and set aside.

4 Mix the ingredients for the sauce (except for the oil) until smooth, then add the reserved pineapple sirup. Cook, stirring continuously, over gentle heat until the sauce boils and becomes thick.

5 Heat the 3 tablespoons oil in a large skillet. Add the vegetables and pineapple. Cook over high heat for 3–4 minutes, stirring frequently.

6 Heat the oil for deep frying to 350 F and cook the noodles in it, a few at a time, until crisp. Drain on absorbent paper, break up and arrange on a dish.

7 Put the vegetables on top of the noodles and pour the sauce over them. Serve immediately.

Manchurian Vegetables

Serves 4–6

7 cups cabbage, finely shredded
or grated
$1\frac{1}{4}$ cups carrots, grated
1 onion, grated
2 tablespoons cornstarch
5 tablespoons all-purpose flour
3–4 cloves garlic, finely chopped
1 green chili, chopped
salt to taste
2 pinches ground black pepper
$\frac{1}{4}$ teaspoon monosodium glutamate

oil for deep frying
SAUCE
2 tablespoons oil
1 tablespoon finely chopped garlic
1 tablespoon finely chopped green
chilies
4 tablespoons soy sauce
1 tablespoon cornstarch
$\frac{2}{3}$ cup water
pinch of monosodium glutamate

1 Mix the cabbage, carrots, onion, cornstarch, flour, garlic, chopped chili, salt, pepper and monosodium glutamate. Shape spoonfuls of the mixture into balls about the size of small eggs, then flatten them slightly.

2 Heat the oil for deep frying to 350 F and fry the vegetable balls a few at a time until golden brown. Drain on absorbent paper and keep hot.

3 To make the sauce, heat the oil, add the garlic with the chopped chilies and fry for a few seconds.

4 Mix the soy sauce and cornstarch with a little of the water. Add the remaining water and pour the mixture into the pan with the garlic and chilies. Bring to the boil, simmer for 1 minute, then add the monosodium glutamate and a little salt.

5 Arrange the vegetable balls on a serving dish, pour the hot sauce over and serve immediately.

Masala Potatoes with Peas

Serves 2

$\frac{1}{2}$ fresh coconut
$2\frac{1}{2}$ cups water
2 teaspoons coriander seeds
1 teaspoon cumin seeds
2 teaspoons poppy seeds
6–7 mild red chilies
1-in piece fresh root ginger, grated
6 cloves garlic, pressed
1 large onion, chopped

$\frac{1}{4}$ cup ghee
2 tomatoes, chopped
2 cups peas
2 large potatoes, cut into cubes
salt to taste
$\frac{1}{2}$ teaspoon sugar
1 tablespoon chopped fresh
coriander leaves

1 To make coconut milk, remove all the coconut from its shell and grate coarsely. Reserve 1 tablespoon of the grated coconut. Place the remainder in a bowl and add 2 cups of the water, then allow to stand for about 30 minutes.

2 Grind the coriander, cumin and poppy seeds with the chilies, reserved coconut, ginger, garlic and onion to form a paste.

3 Melt the ghee in a saucepan, add the paste and fry for a few minutes. Add the chopped tomatoes and cook for 2 minutes. Stir in the peas and potatoes and continue to fry for a further 2 minutes.

4 Add 1 cup of coconut milk, the remaining water and salt. Bring just to the boil, reduce the heat and simmer, covered, until the vegetables are tender – about 20 minutes.

5 Stir in the remaining coconut milk and the sugar. Heat through, then sprinkle the chopped coriander on top and serve immediately with hot parathas (page 80).

Moglai Potatoes

(Illustrated on pages 24/25)

Serves 4

10–12 new potatoes or small mature
potatoes
4 cloves
2–3 teaspoons poppy seeds
2 green cardamoms
2 green chilies
$\frac{1}{2}$-in piece fresh root ginger, grated
3 cloves garlic
$\frac{2}{3}$ cup yogurt
salt to taste

$\frac{1}{4}$ cup ghee
2 onions, grated
1 teaspoon ground coriander
1 teaspoon ground cumin
1 teaspoon chili powder
$\frac{1}{4}$ teaspoon turmeric
2 cups water
1 cup peas
2 tablespoons light cream
$\frac{1}{2}$ teaspoon sugar

1 Scrub, scrape or pare the potatoes, then prick them thoroughly using a cocktail stick. Place the potatoes in a basin, cover with cold water and allow to soak for about 10 minutes.

2 Grind the cloves, poppy seeds, cardamoms, chilies, ginger and garlic to a paste.

3 Drain the potatoes, then mix them with the yogurt, paste and salt. Allow to stand for 1 hour.

4 Melt the ghee in a heavy-based saucepan and fry the grated onion in it for a few minutes. Add the coriander, cumin, chili powder and turmeric. Continue to fry for 2–3 minutes.

5 Stir in the potato mixture and water, heat to simmering point and cook, uncovered, until the potatoes are tender. This should take about 15–20 minutes.

6 Add the peas, cream and sugar, stir well and cook for a few minutes until the peas are tender, then serve hot.

Note: If you like, you can first fry the potatoes in ghee until golden brown all over.

Pea and Potato Patties

(Illustrated on page 29)

Serves 4–6

BATTER
$\frac{1}{2}$ cup all-purpose flour
salt to taste
$\frac{3}{4}$ cup plus 2 tablespoons water
PATTIES
small bunch of fresh coriander
leaves, trimmed
3 green chilies, chopped
1 tablespoon grated fresh coconut
$\frac{1}{2}$ teaspoon sugar
$\frac{1}{2}$ teaspoon salt
2 cups peas, cooked
$4\frac{1}{2}$ cups potato, boiled, cooled and
grated

2 tablespoons cornstarch
juice of $\frac{1}{2}$ lemon
a little all-purpose flour
SAUCE
2 tomatoes
2 tablespoons ghee
1 onion, grated
$\frac{1}{4}-\frac{1}{2}$ teaspoon chili powder
2 tablespoons tomato purée
1 cup water
oil for deep frying

1 Make a thin batter by sifting the flour into a bowl with a little salt, gradually beating in the water until smooth. Allow to stand.

2 Grind the trimmed coriander leaves with two of the chilies, coconut, half the sugar and $\frac{1}{2}$ teaspoon salt to make a paste.

3 Mash the peas with the paste, remaining sugar and $\frac{1}{2}$ teaspoon salt.

4 Mix the potatoes with the cornstarch, lemon juice, remaining chili and salt to taste.

5 Take a spoonful of the potato mixture and knead it into a ball about the size of a small egg. Flatten the mixture in the palm of your hand to give a small patty.

6 Place a spoonful of the mashed peas in the middle of the patty, then bring the potato mixture up around it to form a ball. Flatten the ball to make a neat potato patty, enclosing the pea mixture, and lightly coat it with flour.

7 Place the tomatoes in a bowl, cover with boiling water and allow to stand for 1 minute. Drain, skin and finely chop.

8 Heat the ghee in a saucepan, add the onion and cook until golden brown. Stir in the tomato pulp, chili powder and salt to taste, then add the tomato purée and water. Bring to the boil, cover and simmer steadily for 20 minutes.

9 Heat the oil for deep frying to 350 F. Dip the patties in the batter then deep fry them until crisp and golden. Drain on absorbent paper.

10 Place the halved cooked patties on a serving platter and pour the hot sauce over them. Serve immediately.

Green Peas Ambti

Serves 6

5 tablespoons oil
1 large onion, chopped
2 tablespoons grated coconut
2 teaspoons coriander seeds
3 cinnamon sticks
1 teaspoon cumin seeds
3 cloves
3 peppercorns
6 red chilies

6 cloves garlic
4 cups peas
$1\frac{1}{4}$ cups water
salt to taste
3–4 tablespoons tamarind water or 2
teaspoons tamarind paste
chopped fresh coriander leaves to
garnish

1 Heat 2 tablespoons of the oil in a skillet and fry the onion with the coconut, coriander, cinnamon sticks, cumin seeds, cloves, peppercorns and chilies for at least 3–4 minutes. Grind all these fried ingredients together with the garlic to make a paste.

2 Heat the remaining oil in a saucepan, add the peas, paste, water and salt. Stir in the tamarind water or tamarind paste and bring to the boil. Reduce the heat and simmer for about 15 minutes or until the peas are cooked.

3 Serve hot garnished with the chopped fresh coriander.

Note: Tamarind water can be made by soaking 1 tablespoon chopped tamarind in 3–4 tablespoons water. Allow to stand for about 1 hour, then strain through a sieve.

Masala Corn with Peas

Serves 4

2 large tomatoes	$\frac{1}{4}$ cup ghee
2 teaspoons coriander seeds	2 cups peas
1 teaspoon cumin seeds	2 cups frozen corn
2 cinnamon sticks	$1\frac{1}{4}$ cups water
2 cloves	$\frac{1}{2}$ teaspoon sugar
10–12 red chilies	salt to taste
1-in piece fresh root ginger, grated	1 cup milk
5 cloves garlic	5 tablespoons yogurt
2 large onions, chopped	2 tablespoons ground poppy seeds

1 Put the tomatoes in a bowl and pour over enough boiling water to cover them. Allow to stand for 1 minute, then drain and skin them. Grate the tomatoes into a bowl.

2 Grind the coriander and cumin seeds with the cinnamon, cloves, chilies, ginger, garlic and chopped onions to make a paste.

3 Melt the ghee and fry the paste in it for 3–4 minutes. Add the grated tomatoes and cook for a few minutes.

4 Add the peas, corn, water, sugar and salt and continue to cook for a few minutes.

5 Mix the milk, yogurt and ground poppy seeds, then stir this mixture into the vegetables. Bring to the boil, boil for 5 minutes and serve hot.

Spicy Corn

(Illustrated on pages 52/53)

Serves 4–6

2 tablespoons ghee or butter	$\frac{2}{3}$ cup light cream
1 onion, chopped	$\frac{2}{3}$ cup yogurt
4 green chilies, chopped	3 tablespoons chopped fresh
4 cups corn	coriander leaves
salt to taste	

1 Melt the ghee or butter in a saucepan and fry the onion in it for a few minutes until soft. Add the chilies and fry for a few seconds.

2 Stir in the corn and salt to taste. Cook for a few minutes, stirring frequently until the corn is hot. Add the cream, yogurt and chopped coriander. Cook gently until hot, then serve immediately.

Corn Curry

Serves 4

1 fresh coconut	2 tablespoons ghee
$3\frac{3}{4}$ cups water	2 cinnamon sticks
1 onion, chopped	2 cloves
large bunch of fresh coriander	2 green cardamoms
leaves, trimmed	juice of $\frac{1}{2}$ lemon
6 green chilies	3 cups frozen corn
7 cloves garlic	salt to taste
4 teaspoons poppy seeds	lemon wedges to garnish
1-in piece fresh root ginger	

1 Pierce two of the eyes in the top of the coconut, then drain out the coconut water and reserve it for another use. Break open the nut with a hammer, remove and grate the flesh. Reserve 1 tablespoon of the grated coconut.

2 To make coconut milk, place the grated coconut in a bowl, pour in the water and allow to stand for about 30 minutes. Chop the coconut and water in a blender, then strain through a sieve.

3 Grind the onion with the coriander leaves, chilies, garlic, poppy seeds, ginger and reserved coconut until the ingredients are reduced to a paste.

4 Melt the ghee in a heavy-based saucepan and fry the paste in it for 2 minutes. Add the cinnamon, cloves and cardamoms, continue to fry for a few minutes, then stir in the lemon juice.

5 Add the corn, coconut milk and salt, mix well and simmer for about 10 minutes, until the corn is cooked. Serve hot, with wedges of lemon to garnish. Squeeze the lemon juice over the curry before eating it.

Masala Corn

Serves 4

8–10 pickling onions	1 green or red pepper, chopped
ghee for deep frying	1 tomato, chopped
10–12 small new potatoes	1 teaspoon chili powder
7 green chilies	3 cups corn, cooked
2 onions, chopped	3 teaspoons vinegar
1-in piece fresh root ginger, grated	salt to taste
3 tablespoons oil	scallions to garnish

1 Boil the pickling onions in salted water until tender.

2 Heat the ghee for deep frying to 350F. Add the potatoes and cook until golden. Drain on absorbent paper.

3 Grind four of the chilies to a paste with half the chopped onion and the ginger.

4 Heat the oil in a saucepan and fry the remaining chopped onion for a few minutes. Add the paste and continue to fry for a few minutes.

5 Stir in the pepper, tomato and chili powder and fry for at least 3–4 minutes. Chop the remaining chilies.

6 Add the corn, cooked onions, potatoes, vinegar, chopped chilies and salt to taste. Cook, stirring occasionally, until all the ingredients are hot.

7 Chop the scallions and sprinkle over the masala. Serve immediately.

Masala Gobhi

(Illustrated on pages 104/105)

Serves 4

2 lb cauliflower	1 teaspoon ground coriander
ghee or oil for deep frying	1 teaspoon ground cumin
3 large tomatoes, quartered	1 lb new, or small mature, potatoes,
$\frac{2}{3}$ cup water	boiled
$\frac{1}{4}$ cup ghee	1 cup peas
3 large onions, grated	salt to taste
5 cloves garlic	3 tablespoons light cream
1-in piece fresh root ginger, grated	$\frac{1}{2}$ teaspoon sugar
$\frac{1}{2}$ teaspoon garam masala (page 124)	chopped fresh coriander leaves to
2 teaspoons chili powder	garnish

1 Break the cauliflower into large florets. Heat the ghee or oil for deep frying to 350F, add the cauliflower, a few florets at a time, and cook until golden. Drain on absorbent paper.

2 Place the tomatoes in a saucepan, add the water and bring to the boil. Cover the pan, reduce the heat and simmer for 5 minutes. Strain through a sieve.

3 Melt the $\frac{1}{4}$ cup ghee, add the grated onions and fry until lightly colored. Meanwhile, grind the garlic and ginger together to make a paste.

4 Stir the paste, garam masala, chili powder, coriander and cumin into the fried onions and continue to cook for 1 minute.

5 Add the cauliflower, potatoes, peas, salt to taste and tomato stock, then cook for about 5 minutes to reheat all the vegetables and cook the peas.

6 Finally, stir in the cream and sugar and serve immediately, sprinkled with the chopped coriander leaves.

Vegetable Kheema

Serves 4

3 large tomatoes
5 green chilies, chopped
6–7 cloves garlic
$\frac{1}{2}$-in piece fresh root ginger, grated
3 cloves
3 green cardamoms
8–10 peppercorns
1 teaspoon cumin seeds
$1\frac{1}{2}$ teaspoons chili powder
5–6 tablespoons oil

4 onions, finely chopped
2 lb cauliflower, trimmed and
coarsely grated
$\frac{1}{4}$ teaspoon turmeric
$\frac{2}{3}$ cup water
$\frac{1}{2}$ cup crumbled paneer (page 122);
or khoya (page 123)
salt to taste
1 tablespoon chopped fresh
coriander leaves

1 Put the tomatoes in a bowl and cover with boiling water. Allow to stand for 1 minute, then skin and grate them into a pulp.

2 Grind the chilies with the garlic, ginger, cloves, cardamoms, peppercorns, cumin seeds and chili powder to make a paste.

3 Heat the oil in a saucepan and fry the onions in it until golden in color. Add the paste and continue to fry for 3–4 minutes.

4 Add the grated cauliflower, turmeric and water. Bring to the boil, reduce the heat, then cover and cook for 10–12 minutes.

5 Uncover the pan and continue to simmer, stirring continuously, for about 2–3 minutes.

6 Add the crumbled paneer or khoya to the pan and mix well. Finally, add the tomato pulp and salt. Cook until the oil floats – about 5 minutes.

7 Sprinkle the coriander over and serve hot with parathas (page 80).

Eggplant in Chili-garlic Sauce

(Illustrated on pages 56/57)

Serves 4–6

3 long eggplant
3 scallions
$\frac{1}{4}$ teaspoon monosodium glutamate
CHILI-GARLIC SAUCE
1 cup tomato catsup or
tomato purée
1 teaspoon chili oil
4 teaspoons chili sauce

$\frac{1}{2}$ teaspoon finely grated fresh root
ginger
1 clove garlic, pressed
1 teaspoon sugar
salt to taste
oil for deep frying
3 tablespoons oil

1 You can peel the eggplant if you like, then cut them lengthwise into eighths. Chop the scallions and mix them with the monosodium glutamate.

2 Mix all the ingredients for the chili-garlic sauce and make sure they are thoroughly combined.

3 Heat the oil for deep frying, add the eggplant and cook until soft. Drain on absorbent paper.

4 Heat the 3 tablespoons oil in a large skillet. Add the scallion mixture and cook for 1 minute. Add the eggplant and pour in the chili sauce.

5 Cook gently until the eggplant is hot, then serve immediately.

Note: To make chili oil, chop 4–5 red chilies and add them to 5 tablespoons heated oil. Allow to cool, then leave to stand for at least 2 hours. Store in an airtight bottle.

Stuffed Pumpkin

Serves 8

1 medium pumpkin
salt to taste
$\frac{1}{4}$ lb green beans
2 medium carrots
4 tablespoons oil
$\frac{1}{2}$ teaspoon mustard seeds
2 cups peas
3 teaspoons chili powder
about $\frac{1}{2}$ teaspoon turmeric

2 teaspoons ground coriander
2 teaspoons ground cumin
1 tablespoon chopped fresh
coriander leaves
1 tablespoon grated fresh coconut
2 onions, grated
2 tomatoes, finely chopped
1 cup yogurt
$\frac{3}{4}$ cup water

1 Lightly peel the pumpkin and cut in half. Scoop out the seeds from both portions and sprinkle salt on the inside. Finely chop the green beans and carrots.

2 Heat half the oil in a saucepan and fry the mustard seeds in it for $\frac{1}{2}$ minute.

3 Add the chopped vegetables, peas, half the chili powder, $\frac{1}{4}$ teaspoon of the turmeric, 1 teaspoon each of the coriander and cumin and salt to taste. Cover and cook gently until the vegetables are soft – about 15–20 minutes.

4 Stir in the chopped coriander leaves and grated coconut. Stuff the pumpkin halves with this vegetable mixture and place them in a large ovenproof dish or roasting pan.

5 Heat the remaining oil in a small saucepan, add the grated onions and fry until they are lightly colored. Add the remaining coriander, cumin, chili powder and a pinch of turmeric, then fry for a further $\frac{1}{2}$ minute. Stir in the tomatoes and cook for 3–4 minutes. Stir in the yogurt and salt to taste. Cook gently for 1 minute, then pour in the water.

6 Pour the sauce over the pumpkin halves, cover loosely with foil and cook in a moderately hot oven (400 F) for about 45 minutes or until the pumpkin is tender. Serve hot.

Bread Koftas in Pumpkin Curry

(Illustrated on pages 92/93)

Serves 4

KOFTAS
6 thick slices bread
5 tablespoons yogurt
3 tablespoons all-purpose flour
1 tablespoon chopped fresh
coriander leaves
4 green chilies, chopped
2 pinches baking soda
salt to taste
oil for deep frying
PUMPKIN CURRY
8 small new or mature potatoes,
boiled
1 small pumpkin

2 cups water
2 large tomatoes
$\frac{1}{4}$ cup ghee
3 onions, grated
1 tablespoon chili powder
$1\frac{1}{2}$ teaspoons ground coriander
$1\frac{1}{2}$ teaspoons ground cumin
$\frac{1}{4}$ teaspoon turmeric
2 teaspoons Punjabi garam masala
(page 124)
1 cup yogurt
$\frac{1}{2}$ cup peas
salt to taste

1 First prepare the koftas. Remove the crusts from the bread slices, break the slices into pieces and place in a bowl. Pour the yogurt over the bread and leave to soak for 20 minutes.

2 Add the flour, chopped coriander, chilies, baking soda and salt to taste. Mix the ingredients thoroughly with a wooden spoon. Shape small spoonfuls of the mixture into balls about the size of walnuts.

3 Heat the oil for deep frying to 350 F, then fry the koftas a few at a time until golden brown. Drain on absorbent paper. While the oil is hot, deep fry the potatoes for the pumpkin curry until golden brown. Drain on absorbent paper and set aside.

4 Peel the pumpkin and cut the flesh into 1-in cubes and place in a saucepan. Add about three-quarters of the water and bring to the boil. Reduce the heat and simmer, covered, for about 30 minutes or until the pumpkin is tender. Cool slightly then purée in a blender until smooth.

5 Put the tomatoes in a bowl, pour over boiling water to cover and allow to stand for 1 minute. Skin and grate the tomatoes so that they form a pulp.

6 Melt the ghee in a saucepan and fry the grated onions in it until light brown in color. Add the chili powder, coriander, cumin, turmeric and garam masala. Continue to fry for a few seconds.

7 Pour in the yogurt, pumpkin and tomato pulps, then add the remaining water and cook for a few minutes. Add the peas, fried potatoes and salt to taste, then cook gently until the peas are cooked and the potatoes are hot.

8 Add the koftas to the curry, bring to the boil so that the koftas are hot and serve immediately.

Paneer Mutter Korma

(Illustrated on page 81)

Serves 4

2½ cups paneer (page 122)
ghee or oil for deep frying
1 tablespoon poppy seeds
1 tablespoon chopped cashew nuts
2 tablespoons milk
1-in piece fresh root ginger, grated
5 cloves garlic
¼ cup ghee
3 onions, grated
2 cinnamon sticks
2 bay leaves
2 cloves
1 teaspoon chili powder

2½ cups water
4 tomatoes, chopped
1 cup yogurt
1½ teaspoons freshly ground garam
masala (page 124)
2 teaspoons freshly ground roasted
cumin seeds
1 teaspoon ground coriander
1 cup peas
2 tablespoons light cream
1 teaspoon sugar
salt to taste

1 Cut half the paneer into cubes and crumble the remainder.

2 Heat the ghee or oil for deep frying to 350F, then fry the paneer cubes until golden. Drain carefully on absorbent paper.

3 Place the poppy seeds and cashew nuts in a small bowl and add the milk. Leave to soak for 30 minutes, then grind to a paste with the ginger and garlic.

4 Melt the ¼ cup ghee and fry the grated onions in it until lightly colored. Add the cinnamon, bay leaves and cloves, then fry for a few minutes. Stir in the chili powder and half the water, then continue to cook for 1 minute.

5 Place the tomatoes in a saucepan with a little water. Bring to the boil, cook for a few minutes, then purée in a blender and strain through a sieve. Add to the onion mixture and bring to the boil.

6 Stir in the yogurt, then add the garam masala, ground cumin, coriander and the paste. Cook gently for a few minutes. Add the remaining water, peas and the fried paneer. Bring to the boil and boil for 2 minutes.

7 Finally, add the crumbled paneer, fresh cream, sugar and salt. Stir carefully, then serve hot.

Note: To roast cumin seeds, or other whole spices, place them in a heavy-based skillet and cook over medium heat, stirring continuously, until the seeds pop and change color. Remove the roasted seeds from the pan immediately so that they do not overcook and become bitter.

Baked Paneer Mutter

Serves 4

3 large tomatoes
6 cloves garlic
1-in piece fresh root ginger, grated
8 mild red chilies
1 tablespoon chopped cashew nuts
1 tablespoon poppy seeds
2 teaspoons coriander seeds
1 teaspoon cumin seeds
$\frac{1}{4}$ cup ghee

4 cups peas
salt to taste
1 tablespoon light cream
$\frac{1}{2}$ teaspoon sugar
2 tablespoons butter
1 tablespoon all-purpose flour
$1\frac{1}{4}$ cups milk
1 cup paneer (page 122)
2 green chilies, chopped

1 Roughly chop the tomatoes and place them in a saucepan. Add 1 tablespoon water and cook until they form a pulp. Strain through a sieve.

2 Grind the garlic, ginger, red chilies, cashew nuts, poppy, coriander and cumin seeds to make a paste.

3 Melt the ghee and fry the paste for 2–3 minutes. Add the tomato pulp, peas and salt, stir well, then cook for a few minutes. Add the cream and sugar.

4 Melt the butter in a saucepan, add the flour and cook, stirring, for a minute. Gradually pour in the milk, stirring continuously over low heat until the sauce boils and thickens.

5 Cut the paneer into cubes, mix in the green chilies and salt to taste, then stir both into the sauce.

6 Spoon the pea mixture into a greased ovenproof dish and top with the paneer mixture. Bake in a hot oven (450F) for 20 minutes, until browned on top. Serve immediately.

Baked Paneer with Chutney

Serves 4

$2\frac{1}{2}$ cups paneer (page 122)
large bunch of fresh coriander
leaves, trimmed
4 green chilies
3 tablespoons grated fresh coconut

$\frac{3}{4}$ teaspoon sugar
juice of $\frac{1}{2}$ lemon
salt to taste
2 tablespoons thick yogurt

1 Cut the paneer into $\frac{1}{2}$-in cubes. Place them on foil on a cookie sheet.

2 Grind the coriander, chilies, coconut, sugar, lemon juice and salt to taste to make a paste. Mix the yogurt into the paste and spread the mixture over the paneer cubes.

3 Wrap the foil around the paneer and bake in a moderately hot oven (400F) for 15 minutes. Serve hot.

Note: Home-made paneer can be fried and baked without melting. The prepared cheese can be stored in the refrigerator for about a week but if you do not have the time to make paneer, then certain cream cheeses can also be cooked successfully. However, most soft cream cheeses melt when heated so use firm, full fat soft cheese.

Yogurt Kofta Curry

(Illustrated on pages 88/89)

Serves 4

KOFTAS
$\frac{2}{3}$ cup yogurt
$\frac{3}{4}$ cup gram flour
2 tablespoons chopped fresh
coriander leaves
6 green chilies, chopped
1 teaspoon cumin seeds
2 pinches baking soda
salt to taste
PASTE
2 teaspoons coriander seeds
1 teaspoon cumin seeds
2 teaspoons poppy seeds
1 onion, chopped
4 cloves garlic

1-in piece fresh root ginger, grated
2 green chilies
1 tablespoon chopped fresh
coriander leaves
$\frac{1}{4}$ teaspoon turmeric
SAUCE
2 large tomatoes
$1\frac{1}{4}$ cups water
$\frac{1}{4}$ cup ghee
5 tablespoons milk
salt to taste
2 tablespoons light cream
$\frac{1}{2}$ teaspoon sugar
oil or ghee for deep frying

1 Mix all the ingredients for the koftas to make a thick batter.

2 Grind the coriander, cumin and poppy seeds with the onion, garlic, ginger, chilies, chopped coriander and turmeric to make a paste.

3 Roughly chop the tomatoes for the sauce and place them in a small saucepan with about three-quarters of the water. Bring to the boil, then reduce the heat and simmer for 15 minutes. Strain through a sieve or purée the tomatoes and water in a blender, then strain through a sieve.

4 Melt the $\frac{1}{4}$ cup ghee in a saucepan. Add the paste and cook for 3–4 minutes, stirring frequently to prevent it sticking to the pan.

5 Stir in the blended tomatoes, milk, salt and remaining water. Bring to the boil and boil steadily for 10 minutes.

6 Meanwhile, heat the oil or ghee for deep frying to 350 F. Drop spoonfuls of the kofta mixture into the hot oil, then fry until golden brown. Drain carefully on absorbent paper.

7 Stir the cream into the sauce and add the sugar. Carefully add the koftas and serve immediately with plain cooked rice or parathas (page 80).

Paneer Makhani

(Illustrated on pages 20/21)

Serves 2

1 cup paneer (page 122)
ghee or oil for deep frying
2 tablespoons yogurt
3 large tomatoes
$\frac{1}{3}$ cup ghee
3 onions, grated
1 teaspoon garam masala (page 124)
1 teaspoon ground coriander
1 teaspoon ground cumin

$1\frac{1}{2}$ teaspoons chili powder
$\frac{1}{4}$ teaspoon turmeric
salt to taste
1 cup water
$\frac{2}{3}$ cup light cream
1 tablespoon butter
chopped fresh coriander leaves to
garnish

1 Cut the paneer into fingers. Heat the ghee or oil for deep frying to 350 F, then add the paneer fingers, a few at a time, and cook until golden.

2 Carefully drain the fried paneer on absorbent paper, then transfer them to a plate and pour the yogurt over the fingers.

3 Place the tomatoes in a bowl, pour over boiling water to cover and allow to stand for 1 minute. Drain and skin the tomatoes, then chop them finely.

4 Melt the $\frac{1}{3}$ cup ghee and fry the onions in it until lightly colored. Add the garam masala, coriander, cumin, chili powder, turmeric and salt. Fry for 1 minute. Stir in the chopped tomatoes, and continue to fry for at least 5 minutes or until the ghee floats.

5 Pour in the water, bring to the boil, then reduce the heat and add the cream. Cook for a few minutes, then stir in the butter. Add the fried paneer and yogurt, heat through and garnish with the chopped coriander. Serve hot.

Dal Dishes

Dals are split pulses: dried beans and lentils. This chapter contains recipes for the whole pulses as well as the split dals. Rich in protein, these ingredients are most important in a vegetarian diet; served with rice and bread they make a complete and nourishing meal.

Dried beans should be stored in airtight containers but, although they do have a remarkably long shelf life, remember that you cannot store them forever. Before you cook the pulses, carefully sort through them and discard any that are discolored, at the same time throw away any small bits of grit or dirt which may be mixed up with them. To clean the dals or beans, rinse them under running water, then cover them with cold water and leave to soak overnight. Next day, drain the beans and throw away any that are wrinkled and have not absorbed the water.

When cooked, you will find that the mild flavor of the pulses is readily influenced by the addition of spices and other well-flavored ingredients in a variety of delicious dishes.

Masala Dal

(Illustrated on page 100)

Serves 4

$\frac{1}{2}$ cup moong dal
$\frac{1}{2}$ cup masoor dal
$\frac{1}{2}$ cup urad dal
$\frac{1}{2}$ cup toovar dal
5 cups water
2 teaspoons coriander seeds
1 teaspoon cumin seeds
8 mild red chilies
$\frac{1}{4}$ teaspoon turmeric
3 cinnamon sticks
3 peppercorns

3 cloves
5 cloves garlic, crushed
1-in piece fresh root ginger, grated
1 tablespoon chopped fresh
coriander leaves
$\frac{1}{4}$ cup ghee
3 onions, grated
2 tomatoes, chopped
salt to taste
fresh coriander leaves to garnish

1 Place all the dals in a colander and wash them thoroughly under running water. Place the dals in a saucepan. Add the water and bring to the boil. Cover the pan, reduce the heat and cook for about 50 minutes, or until the water has been absorbed.

2 Meanwhile, grind the coriander and cumin seeds with the chilies, turmeric, cinnamon, peppercorns, cloves, garlic, ginger and chopped coriander leaves to form a paste.

3 Melt the ghee, add the grated onions and fry until lightly colored. Stir in the paste and continue to fry for 3–4 minutes. Add the chopped tomatoes and cook for a further 3–4 minutes.

4 Finally, add the cooked dals and salt, stirring to combine all the ingredients. Cook for 5–7 minutes, then serve hot garnished with coriander leaves.

Rajma Curry

(Illustrated on page 85)

DAL DISHES

Serves 4–6

1¼ cups red kidney beans	1 lb tomatoes
7 cloves garlic	2 cups water
7 green chilies, chopped	2 teaspoons sugar
1-in piece fresh root ginger, grated	salt to taste
¼ cup ghee	2 tablespoons chopped fresh
2 onions, grated	coriander leaves (optional)
1 teaspoon chili powder	

1 Soak the red kidney beans overnight.

2 Drain the beans, put them in a saucepan with enough water to come at least 1 in over the top of the beans and bring to the boil. *Boil for 3 minutes*, then reduce the heat, cover the pan and simmer for about 45 minutes, until the beans are tender. Check that the water level has not fallen below the beans during cooking and add more boiling water if necessary.

3 Meanwhile, grind the garlic, chilies and ginger to a paste.

4 Melt the ghee, add the grated onions and fry for 2–3 minutes. Add the paste and chili powder and continue to fry for 1 minute. Add the drained cooked beans.

5 Cut the tomatoes into quarters and place them in a saucepan with the water. Bring to the boil, reduce the heat and simmer for 5 minutes. Strain through a sieve to give a tomato stock.

6 Add the tomato stock to the beans with the sugar and salt. Cook, stirring, for a few minutes and serve hot, sprinkled with chopped coriander if you like.

Overleaf *From the left: Spicy Corn (page 37), Bean Hotpot (page 55), Cabbage Wadas (page 107) and Poppadums (page 77)*

Broad Bean Curry

Serves 4–6

2 cups dried broad beans
4 tomatoes
$\frac{2}{3}$ cup water
2 onions
5–6 cloves garlic
6 mild red chilies
3 teaspoons coriander seeds

1 teaspoon cumin seeds
2 teaspoons poppy seeds
4–5 peppercorns
4–5 cloves
2–3 cinnamon sticks
2 tablespoons ghee
salt to taste

1 Soak the beans overnight.

2 Place the drained beans in a saucepan and pour in enough water to come about 1 in over the top of the beans. Bring to the boil, reduce the heat and cover the pan, then simmer for about 45 minutes or until the beans are tender.

3 Cut the tomatoes into quarters and place them in a saucepan with the water. Bring to the boil, reduce the heat and simmer for 5 minutes. Strain through a sieve.

4 Roast the unskinned onions over a gas flame or under a hot broiler until black. Cool slightly, then remove the skin and grind the flesh to a paste with all the remaining ingredients except for the ghee and salt.

5 Melt the ghee in a heavy-based saucepan and fry the paste in it for 3–4 minutes. Add the drained, cooked beans, tomato stock and salt. Stir well, then cook for a few minutes. Serve hot with parathas (page 80).

Bean Hotpot

(Illustrated on back cover and pages 52/53)

Serves 4

½ cup dried broad beans
⅓ cup red kidney beans
½ cup black beans
2 lb tomatoes
1 tablespoon ghee
1 onion, chopped
1 teaspoon chili powder
2–3 teaspoons sugar
salt to taste

5–6 green chilies
2 thick slices bread
1 tablespoon chopped cashew nuts
or peanuts
1 tablespoon chopped fresh
coriander leaves
1 teaspoon lemon juice
4 potatoes, boiled and mashed
oil for deep frying

1 Soak all the beans together overnight. Drain and place them in a saucepan. Add enough cold water to come about 2 in over the top of the beans. Bring to the boil, *boil for 3 minutes*, then reduce the heat and cover the pan. Simmer for about 1½ hours or until the beans are tender.

2 Cut the tomatoes into quarters and place them in a saucepan. Add 2 tablespoons water and cook gently until the tomatoes are soft and pulpy – about 20 minutes. When cooked, strain through a sieve.

3 Melt the ghee in a saucepan and fry the onion in it for 1 minute. Add the tomato pulp, chili powder, sugar and salt to taste, and the drained beans. Split two of the chilies and add them to the pan. Bring to the boil and cook for about 10–15 minutes.

4 Remove the crusts from the bread, then quickly dip the slices in water. Squeeze out and crumble the bread. Mix the bread with the nuts, chopped coriander and lemon juice.

5 Chop the remaining chilies and add them to the mashed potatoes with the bread mixture. Make sure the ingredients are thoroughly combined and add salt to taste.

6 Shape the mixture into small balls about the size of walnuts. Heat the oil for deep frying to 350F, then fry the potato balls until golden. Drain on absorbent paper.

7 Add the potato balls to the bean mixture and serve immediately.

Overleaf *From the left: Eggplant in Chili-garlic Sauce (page 41),
Green Peas Renedy (page 102) and Fruit and
Vegetable Raita (page 76)*

Falafal

(Illustrated on page 61)

Serves 6

1¼ cups chick peas
4 green chilies, roughly chopped
½ teaspoon baking soda
1 tablespoon chopped fresh
coriander leaves
salt to taste
oil for deep frying
HOT SAUCE
2 large tomatoes
10–12 red chilies, roughly chopped
5 cloves garlic
½ teaspoon lemon juice
salt to taste

SESAME SAUCE
2 tablespoons roasted sesame seeds
2 green chilies
4 tablespoons yogurt
½ teaspoon sugar
½ teaspoon mustard powder
SALAD
3 tomatoes, chopped
3 scallions, chopped
4 cups cabbage, shredded
salt to taste
12 pieces pitta bread to serve

1 Soak the chick peas overnight in cold water to cover.

2 Drain and grind the chick peas. Reserve 2 tablespoons of the ground chick peas. Grind the green chilies with the last batch of chick peas and mix in a large bowl with the baking soda.

3 Add the chopped coriander and salt, then knead spoonfuls of the mixture into small balls about the size of walnuts.

4 Heat the oil for deep frying to 350 F and cook the chick pea balls a few at a time until golden brown. Drain on absorbent paper and set aside.

5 To make the hot sauce, start by skinning the tomatoes: place them in a bowl, cover with boiling water and allow to stand for 1 minute. Drain, skin and chop the tomatoes.

6 Mix the tomatoes with the chilies, garlic, lemon juice and salt. Purée these ingredients together in a blender, adding a little water if necessary.

7 Place all the ingredients for the sesame sauce in a blender and add the reserved ground chick peas. Blend until smooth, adding a little water if necessary.

8 Mix the ingredients for the salad and season lightly with salt. Slit the pieces of pitta bread and place a little salad in each. Top with chick pea balls, hot sauce and sesame sauce, then more salad. Serve two pieces of stuffed pitta per person for a filling meal.

Rice Dishes

Rice must be one of the most versatile ingredients and is used in cooking all over the world. Carefully spiced and flavored, the rice is cooked to perfection in the dishes in this chapter – each grain is fluffy yet whole. Basmati rice offers the best flavor in cooking but other long-grain varieties can be used just as well. Pullaos, kormas and baked dishes are included; some are suitable for serving as a light meal on their own, while others make ideal accompaniments.

Mixed with dals, rice goes to make khichadi, a satisfying combination of two main ingredients which complement each other perfectly. Curries are also included with some of these rice dishes, as are vegetables and other flavoring ingredients like coconut. In fact, there is a rice dish suitable for every meal.

Bohri Khichadi

Serves 6

2 cups long-grain rice
1 cup toovar dal
salt to taste
a few saffron strands (optional)
5 red chilies
2 green chilies
2 small onions, chopped
4 cloves garlic

$1\frac{1}{2}$ teaspoons cumin seeds
3 large onions
ghee or oil for deep frying
$\frac{1}{3}$ cup ghee
1 teaspoon garam masala (page 124)
1 cup yogurt
1 teaspoon sugar

1 Cook the rice according to the instructions on page 123 and allow to cool. Cook the dal according to the instructions on page 123. Cool.

2 To make the khichadi, mix the cooked rice and dal, adding salt to taste.

3 Place the saffron (if used) in a small bowl and add a little water. Stand the bowl over hot water and rub the saffron until it dissolves. Add this saffron liquid to the khichadi.

4 Grind the red chilies with the green chilies, chopped small onions, garlic and cumin seeds to make a paste. Chop one of the large onions and slice the remaining onions.

5 Heat the ghee or oil for deep frying to 350F, add the sliced onions, separated into rings, and cook until golden. Drain on absorbent paper and set aside.

6 Melt just over half the $\frac{1}{3}$ cup ghee in a small saucepan. Add the chopped onion and fry for 1 minute. Add the paste and fry for a further 2 minutes. Stir in the garam masala and cook for a few seconds.

7 Remove the pan from the heat. Pour in the yogurt, sugar and salt to taste.

8 Use the remaining ghee to thoroughly grease an ovenproof dish. Place half the fried onion rings in the dish, spread half the khichadi over them and then pour the yogurt mixture over.

9 Mix the remaining onions with the second portion of khichadi and spread this over the yogurt. Cover with foil and bake in a hot oven (450F) for 15 minutes. Serve immediately.

From the top: Falafal (page 58) and Moong Dal Pudas (page 106)

Three-in-one Rice

(Illustrated on pages 92/93)

Serves 6–8

2½ cups long-grain rice
salt to taste
ORANGE RICE
2–3 tomatoes
2 tablespoons ghee
1 onion, chopped
2 carrots, grated
1 teaspoon sugar
2 green chilies, chopped
salt to taste
WHITE RICE
2 tablespoons ghee
½ teaspoon black cumin seeds
2 green chilies, chopped

½ cup paneer (page 122), chopped
salt to taste
GREEN RICE
large bunch of fresh coriander
leaves, trimmed
4 green chilies
4 cloves garlic
1-in piece fresh root ginger, grated
juice of ½ lemon
2 tablespoons ghee
1 onion, chopped
1 cup peas, cooked
salt to taste

1 Cook the rice according to the instructions on page 123, adding salt to taste. Drain (if necessary) and cool. Each grain of cooked rice should be separate.

2 Start by preparing the orange rice. Cut the tomatoes into quarters and place them in a saucepan. Add 2 tablespoons water and bring to the boil. Reduce the heat and cook for 10–15 minutes. Strain the cooked tomatoes through a sieve to make a pulp.

3 Melt the ghee in a saucepan, add the onion and fry for 1 minute. Add the carrots and fry for a further 1 minute.

4 Pour in the tomato pulp, add the sugar, chilies and salt to taste. Cook for 2 minutes, then stir in one-third of the cooked rice. Mix well.

5 In a saucepan, melt the ghee for the white rice. Add the black cumin seeds and cook for a few seconds.

6 Stir in half the remaining rice, chilies and paneer. Add salt to taste and mix well.

7 To make the green rice, start by preparing a paste. Grind the coriander leaves, chilies, garlic, ginger and lemon juice together until fairly smooth.

8 Melt the ghee in a saucepan, add the onion and fry for 1 minute. Add the paste and continue to cook for a further 2 minutes. Stir in the remaining rice and peas, add salt to taste and mix well.

9 Layer the three rice combinations in a greased straight-sided ovenproof baker or firm-based cake pan. Cover closely with foil and stand the container in a large saucepan.

10 Pour enough boiling water into the saucepan to come halfway up the side of the baker or pan. Stand the saucepan over medium heat. Cover the pan and steam the rice dish for 15 minutes.

11 To serve, invert the container on to a serving dish and serve immediately.

Paneer Mutter Pullao

(Illustrated on page 64)

Serves 6

2 cups long-grain rice	4 cloves garlic
salt to taste	7 red chilies
$\frac{1}{2}$ cup ghee	$\frac{1}{2}$-in piece fresh root ginger, grated
$\frac{1}{2}$ teaspoon black cumin seeds	3 teaspoons poppy seeds
2 cinnamon sticks	2 teaspoons coriander seeds
2 cloves	1 teaspoon cumin seeds
ghee or oil for deep frying	3 green cardamoms
$\frac{1}{2}$ lb cauliflower florets	3 cloves
1 cup paneer (page 122), cut into cubes	3 small cinnamon sticks
	$\frac{1}{4}$ teaspoon turmeric
1 cup peas	1 teaspoon salt
PASTE	GARNISH
1 onion, chopped	a few roasted cashew nuts
1 tomato, chopped	chopped fresh coriander leaves

1 Cook the rice according to the instructions on page 123, adding salt to taste, and allow to cool.

2 Melt half the ghee in a saucepan and add the black cumin seeds, cinnamon and cloves. Fry for $\frac{1}{2}$ minute. Add the cooked rice and salt to taste.

3 Heat the ghee or oil for deep frying to 350 F, add the cauliflower florets and cook until golden. Drain on absorbent paper. Cook the paneer in the ghee or oil, then drain carefully. Cook the peas.

4 Grind all the ingredients for the paste until fairly smooth.

5 Heat the remaining ghee in a saucepan and fry the paste for 3 minutes. Add the peas, cauliflower and paneer and mix well. Stir in the rice and mix well, then cook over very low heat for 10 minutes, or until the ingredients are hot.

6 Serve immediately, garnished with the cashew nuts and chopped coriander.

Pullao with Vegetables and Dal

Serves 6

2 cups long-grain rice
salt to taste
1 cup toovar dal
$\frac{1}{4}$ teaspoon saffron strands
2 cups mixed vegetables – for example, green beans, carrots and peas
3 large onions
2 tablespoons grated fresh coconut
8 mild red chilies

1-in piece fresh root ginger, grated
4 cloves garlic
3 teaspoons poppy seeds
3 green cardamoms
2 teaspoons coriander seeds
1 teaspoon cumin seeds
$\frac{1}{4}$ cup ghee
$1\frac{1}{4}$ cups yogurt
1 teaspoon sugar

1 Cook the rice according to the instructions on page 123, adding salt to taste, and allow to cool.

2 Place the toovar dal in a saucepan and add enough water to cover by at least 1 in. Add salt to taste, bring to the boil, then reduce the heat and simmer for about 20 minutes, or until the dal are tender. Drain and cool.

3 Place the saffron in a small bowl, add a little water – about 1 teaspoon – and stand the bowl over hot water. Rub saffron until it dissolves.

4 Prepare the mixed vegetables according to their type, cutting any large ones into bite-sized pieces, and cook in boiling salted water until tender. Chop one of the onions and slice the other two.

5 Grind the chopped onion, coconut, chilies, ginger, garlic, poppy seeds, cardamoms, coriander and cumin seeds to make a paste.

6 Melt the ghee in a skillet. Add the sliced onions and fry them until lightly browned. Remove from the skillet and set aside.

7 Add the paste to the skillet and fry for 3–4 minutes. Remove the skillet from the heat and stir in the yogurt, sugar and salt to taste.

8 Mix the cooked rice and dal with the vegetables, half the fried onion slices, saffron liquid and salt to taste.

9 Grease a straight-sided ovenproof baker. Layer the rice and vegetable mixture in the baker with the yogurt mixture. Top with the remaining sliced onions and cover with foil.

10 Bake in a hot oven (450F) for 20 minutes. Serve hot.

Paneer Mutter Pullao (page 63) and Semolina Pancakes (page 96)

Kashmiri Pullao

Serves 6

2 tablespoons ghee
½ teaspoon black cumin seeds
2 cinnamon sticks
2 cloves
2 green cardamoms
2 bay leaves
2 cups long-grain rice

1¼ cups milk
⅔ cup light cream
1 teaspoon sugar
salt to taste
2 cups water
2 cups mixed fruit, fresh
or canned

1 Melt the ghee in a saucepan, add the cumin seeds and fry for a few minutes. Add the cinnamon, cloves, cardamoms and bay leaves. Stir in the uncooked rice and fry, without adding water, for 2–3 minutes.

2 Add the milk, cream, sugar, salt to taste and the water. Bring to the boil, then reduce the heat so that the rice simmers gently. When the rice is almost cooked, cover the pan and continue to cook very gently until all the liquid is absorbed.

3 Transfer the rice to a serving dish and toss in the fruit. Serve immediately, with curry sauce or with any vegetable curry.

Moglai Pullao

Serves 4

1¼ cups long-grain rice
salt to taste
4 cups mixed vegetables – for
example, carrots, peas and green
beans
⅓ cup ghee
½ teaspoon black cumin seeds
2 small cinnamon sticks
5 green cardamoms

3 cloves garlic
3 green chilies
1 tablespoon poppy seeds
5 cashew nuts
1½ teaspoons coriander seeds
½-in piece fresh root ginger, grated
⅔ cup yogurt
1 teaspoon sugar
1 onion, sliced

1 Cook the rice according to the instructions on page 123, adding salt to taste. Allow to cool. Prepare and cook the vegetables according to their type, cutting any large ones into bite-sized pieces.

2 Heat a quarter of the ghee, add the cumin seeds and fry for a few minutes. Add the cinnamon and two of the cardamoms and fry for a few seconds. Stir in the rice and salt to taste.

3 Grind the garlic, chilies, poppy seeds and remaining cardamoms with the cashew nuts, coriander seeds and ginger to make a paste.

4 Melt half the remaining ghee in a saucepan and fry the paste in it for a few minutes. Remove from the heat, add the yogurt, sugar and salt. Melt the remaining ghee in a skillet and fry the onion for 1 minute.

5 Spread half the rice in the base of an ovenproof dish. Top the rice first with the yogurt mixture, then the vegetables and fried onion. Finally, spread the remaining rice on top.

6 Cover with foil and bake in a hot oven (450F) for 20 minutes. Serve immediately.

Saffron Pullao

(Illustrated on page 81)

Serves 6

$2\frac{1}{2}$ cups long-grain rice	7 cloves garlic
salt to taste	$\frac{1}{4}$ cup ghee
a few saffron strands	3 onions, chopped
1 tablespoon milk	2 teaspoons chili powder
$\frac{1}{2}$ lb green beans	$\frac{1}{2}$ teaspoon turmeric
$\frac{1}{2}$ lb carrots	$\frac{1}{2}$ teaspoon garam masala (page 124)
$\frac{1}{2}$ lb potatoes	2 tablespoons ground coriander
2 cups peas	2 tablespoons ground cumin
1-in piece fresh root ginger, grated	3 tomatoes, chopped

1 Cook the rice according to the instructions on page 123, adding salt to taste, and allow to cool.

2 Place the saffron in a small bowl, add the milk and stand the bowl over hot water. Rub the saffron until it dissolves, then stir into the rice and mix well.

3 Cut the green beans, carrots and potatoes into bite-sized pieces. Cook them in boiling salted water until tender. Cook the peas in the same way. Drain and set aside.

4 Grind the ginger with the garlic to make a paste.

5 Melt the ghee in a saucepan and fry the onions in it until they are light brown in color. Add the paste and fry for 1 minute. Stir in the chili powder, turmeric, garam masala, ground coriander and cumin. Add the tomatoes and cook for a further 2–3 minutes. Add the vegetables and salt to taste, then mix well.

6 Layer the rice and vegetables alternately in an ovenproof dish beginning and ending with rice. Cover with foil and bake in a moderately hot oven (400F) for 30 minutes. Serve hot.

Fruit and Vegetable Pullao

Serves 6

8–10 dried apricots
1 cup paneer (page 122)
3 tablespoons all-purpose flour
pinch of baking soda
salt to taste
2 green chilies, chopped
2 tablespoons chopped fresh
coriander leaves
ghee for deep frying
$1\frac{1}{4}$ cups long-grain rice
$\frac{1}{2}$ cup ghee
$\frac{1}{2}$ teaspoon black cumin seeds
2 cinnamon sticks
2 cloves
2 green cardamoms
1 cup peas

a few saffron strands
a little milk
$1\frac{1}{4}$ cups yogurt
$\frac{1}{2}$ teaspoon sugar
PASTE
1 large onion, chopped
3 tablespoons grated fresh coconut
5 cloves garlic
2 teaspoons coriander seeds
1 teaspoon cumin seeds
2 cinnamon sticks
3 cloves
3 green cardamoms
2 teaspoons poppy seeds
7–8 red chilies
1-in piece fresh root ginger, grated

1 Cut the apricots into small pieces and soak in cold water to cover for 1 hour. Drain.

2 Mix the paneer, flour and baking soda with salt to taste, the chilies and chopped coriander leaves.

3 Heat the ghee for deep frying to 350F. Form spoonfuls of the paneer mixture into balls about the size of walnuts and deep fry until golden brown. Drain these koftas and set aside.

4 Cook the rice according to the instructions on page 123, adding salt to taste, and allow to cool.

5 Melt half the $\frac{1}{2}$ cup ghee in a saucepan. Add the black cumin seeds, cinnamon, cloves and cardamoms and fry for $\frac{1}{2}$ minute. Add the rice, peas and salt to taste. Cook for a few minutes.

6 Warm the saffron with a little milk in a small bowl over hot water. Rub in the saffron until it dissolves. Add to the rice. Stir in the apricot pieces.

7 Mix the yogurt with the sugar and add salt to taste.

8 Grind together all the ingredients for the paste until smooth.

9 Heat the remaining ghee in a small saucepan, add the paste and fry for 3–4 minutes. Remove the pan from the heat and stir in the seasoned yogurt.

10 Add the paneer koftas to the rice and spread one-third of the mixture in a greased ovenproof dish. Spoon half the yogurt sauce over. Arrange half the remaining rice over the sauce.

11 Top first with the remaining sauce, then with the last of the rice. Cover with foil and bake in a hot oven (450F) for 20 minutes. Serve immediately.

Korma Rice

Serves 4–6

$\frac{1}{3}$ cup ghee
2 bay leaves
2 cinnamon sticks
2 green cardamoms
2 cloves
$1\frac{1}{2}$ cups rice
2 pinches turmeric
salt to taste
$3\frac{3}{4}$ cups plus 3 tablespoons water
2 tomatoes
3 cloves garlic
$\frac{1}{2}$-in piece fresh root ginger, grated

4 cups mixed vegetables – for
example, green beans, carrots, peas
and corn
2 onions, grated
$\frac{1}{2}$ teaspoon ground cumin
$\frac{1}{2}$ teaspoon ground coriander
1 teaspoon chili powder
$\frac{1}{2}$ teaspoon sugar
1 tablespoon chopped cashew nuts
1 tablespoon poppy seeds
1 cup milk
2 tablespoons light cream

1 Melt just less than half the ghee in a saucepan, then add the bay leaves, cinnamon, cardamoms and cloves. Cook for $\frac{1}{2}$ minute.

2 Stir in the rice, turmeric, salt to taste and $3\frac{3}{4}$ cups water. Bring to the boil, cover the pan and reduce the heat. Cook for 15–20 minutes or until the rice is tender.

3 When the rice is cooked, drain off the water (if necessary) and cool. Each grain of the cooked rice should be separate.

4 Place the tomatoes in a bowl, cover with boiling water. Allow to stand for 1 minute, then drain, skin and chop.

5 Grind the garlic with the ginger to make a paste.

6 Prepare and cook the mixed vegetables according to their type, cutting any large ones into bite-sized pieces.

7 Melt the remaining ghee and fry the grated onions in it until lightly browned. Add the garlic paste, cumin, coriander and chili powder. Fry for 1 minute. Add the tomatoes and sugar, then fry for a further 3–4 minutes.

8 Stir in the vegetables, 3 tablespoons water and salt to taste. Cook for 2 minutes.

9 Grind the cashew nuts and poppy seeds together, then stir into the milk, add the cream and pour the mixture into the vegetables.

10 Cook for a few minutes, then layer this vegetable korma with the rice in an ovenproof dish. Begin and end with a layer of rice.

11 Bake, covered with foil, in a hot oven (450 F) for 20 minutes. Turn out and serve immediately.

Baked Rice with Green Curry

Serves 4–6

1½ cups long-grain rice
¼ cup ghee
½ teaspoon black cumin seeds
2 cinnamon sticks
2 cloves
salt to taste
large bunch of fresh coriander
leaves, trimmed
7 green chilies
1 onion, chopped
4 cloves garlic
1-in piece fresh root ginger, grated
1 tablespoon chopped fresh mint

1 tablespoon poppy seeds
juice of ½ lemon
2 green cardamoms
1 cup peas
⅔ cup paneer (page 122), cut into
small pieces
⅔ cup yogurt
½ teaspoon sugar
GARNISH (optional)
boiled green peas
potato sticks or lightly crushed
chips

1 Cook the rice according to the instructions on page 123 and allow to cool.

2 Melt half the ghee in a saucepan, add the black cumin seeds, cinnamon and cloves. Fry for ½ minute. Add the rice and salt to taste. Set aside.

3 Grind the coriander leaves, chilies, onion, garlic, ginger, mint, poppy seeds and lemon juice to make a paste.

4 Melt the remaining ghee, add the paste and cardamoms, then fry for 2 minutes and remove from the heat. Add the peas, paneer, yogurt, sugar and salt to taste. Mix well.

5 Layer the two mixtures in a greased ovenproof dish. Make three layers of each, beginning and ending with the rice mixture. Cover with foil and bake in a hot oven (450F) for 20 minutes.

6 Turn the dish upside down on a big serving plate.

7 If liked, surround the baked rice with freshly cooked peas. Sprinkle the potato sticks or chips on the top and sides. Serve hot.

Baked Coconut Rice with Moglai Curry

Serves 4–6

1 fresh coconut
$2\frac{1}{2}$ cups hot water
3 onions, sliced
$\frac{1}{4}$ cup ghee
2 cinnamon sticks
2 cloves
$1\frac{1}{2}$ cups long-grain rice
salt to taste
8 cups mixed vegetables – for
example cauliflower, courgettes,
green beans, carrots and potatoes

3 tomatoes
1 teaspoon finely grated fresh root
ginger
3 cloves garlic, pressed
$\frac{1}{2}$ teaspoon turmeric
2 teaspoons ground coriander
$1\frac{1}{2}$ teaspoons chili powder
1 teaspoon garam masala (page 124)
1 cup milk
3 tablespoons light cream

1 Pierce two of the eyes in the top of the coconut. Drain off the coconut water. Crack the nut open and grate the flesh. Place the grated coconut in a bowl with the hot water and allow to stand for a little while. Chop in a blender and strain through a sieve to make coconut milk.

2 Slice one of the onions and grate the remaining two. Melt half the ghee in a saucepan and fry the sliced onion in it for 1 minute. Add the cinnamon and cloves and fry again for a few minutes.

3 Add the rice, coconut milk and salt to taste. Bring just to the boil, then cover and cook slowly until the rice is cooked – about 20 minutes. Add extra water during cooking if necessary.

4 Prepare and cook the vegetables according to their type. Drain and set aside.

5 Meanwhile, place the tomatoes in a bowl and cover with boiling water. Leave to stand for 1 minute, then skin and chop.

6 Melt the remaining ghee, add the grated onions and fry for a few minutes. Add the ginger and garlic, then fry for $\frac{1}{2}$ minute. Stir in the chopped tomatoes, turmeric, ground coriander, chili powder, garam masala and salt to taste. Fry for at least 3–4 minutes. Add the vegetables, milk and cream and cook for a few minutes.

7 Layer the rice and curry in a greased ovenproof dish, beginning and ending with rice. Cover and bake in a hot oven (450 F) for 20 minutes.

8 Serve hot with fried poppadums (page 77).

Masala Khichadi with Curry Sauce

Serves 6–8

1½ cups masoor dal
2 cups long-grain rice
3 tablespoons grated fresh coconut
5 cloves garlic
2 teaspoons chopped fresh coriander
leaves
1 teaspoon cumin seeds
4 green cardamoms
1-in piece fresh root ginger, grated
6 mild red chilies
½ teaspoon turmeric
¼ cup ghee
salt to taste
CURRY SAUCE
3 large tomatoes
1 teaspoon sugar
salt to taste
1¼ cups water

2 large onions, chopped
1 tablespoon chopped cashew nuts
1 tablespoon chopped almonds
(optional)
1 tablespoon coriander seeds
1 tablespoon poppy seeds
2 teaspoons aniseeds
2 tablespoons grated fresh coconut
1-in piece fresh root ginger
2 green chilies
4 red chilies
3 green cardamoms
3 cloves
3 cinnamon sticks
7 curry leaves
¼ cup ghee
a few saffron strands

1 Soak the masoor dal overnight in enough cold water to cover.

2 Next day, cook the dal according to the instructions on page 123. When cooked, drain and set aside. Meanwhile, cook the rice according to the instructions on page 123. Allow to cool.

3 Grind the coconut with the garlic, chopped coriander, cumin seeds, cardamoms, ginger, chilies and turmeric to make a paste.

4 Melt the ghee in a saucepan, add the paste and cook for 3–4 minutes. To make up the khichadi, add the rice, dal and salt to taste and mix well.

5 To make the curry sauce, cut the tomatoes into quarters and place them in a saucepan with the sugar, salt to taste and water. Bring to the boil and cook until soft and pulpy. Strain through a sieve.

6 Grind all the remaining ingredients except for the ghee and saffron to make a paste.

7 Melt the ghee in a saucepan, add the paste and fry for at least 4 minutes. Add the tomato liquid and heat through.

8 Warm the saffron in a small bowl over hot water. Add a little milk and rub the saffron until it dissolves. Add to the curry sauce. Serve the hot sauce in a dish to accompany the khichadi.

Note: Both the khichadi and the curry sauce can be served as separate dishes.

Side Dishes and Salads

No Indian meal would be complete without a selection of accompaniments, so here are a few recipes for salads and raitas, a chutney and poppadums. Cool Cucumber Salad goes well with hot and spicy vegetable curries. With dry spiced dishes try a moist Fruit and Vegetable Raita or serve Coconut Curry Sauce. Crisp poppadums are the simplest of accompaniments to prepare and they are delicious with all Indian food. Similarly, a bowl of Spicy Yogurt goes very well with most spiced dishes.

When you prepare the recipes in this chapter, look upon them as the final touches to complement the meal. For example, you can serve raitas and salads in small bowls or on attractive platters and where appropriate sprinkle a little chopped fresh coriander or a hint of chili powder over them.

If you have the time, allow yogurt dishes and cool salads to chill lightly before they are served. However, if the vegetable is likely to become watery on standing, as in the case of cucumber, or if any ingredients may discolor, bananas for example, then it's best not to make the dish too far in advance.

Cucumber Salad

(Illustrated on pages 104/105)

Serves 4

2 tablespoons light cream
$\frac{2}{3}$ cup yogurt
1 teaspoon mustard powder

2 green chilies, chopped
salt and sugar to taste
1 large cucumber, finely chopped

1 Mix the cream, yogurt, mustard, chilies, salt and sugar to taste.
2 Stir in the cucumber and chill for 2 hours before serving.

Banana Nut Salad

(Illustrated on page 85)

Serves 6

$\frac{2}{3}$ cup light cream
3 tablespoons yogurt
1 teaspoon mustard powder
salt and sugar to taste
$\frac{1}{4}$ cup paneer (page 122),
crumbled

1 tablespoon chopped roasted
peanuts
6 small bananas
juice of $\frac{1}{2}$ lemon
1 small lettuce, trimmed and washed
2 carrots, grated

1 Mix the cream with the yogurt, mustard, salt and sugar to taste. Stir in the paneer and nuts. Chill for 10 minutes.
2 Slit the bananas lengthwise and sprinkle the lemon juice over them. Arrange the lettuce leaves on a serving dish, lay the bananas on top and pour over the yogurt mixture.
3 Sprinkle the grated carrots on top and serve as an accompaniment with vegetable curries.

Coconut Curry Sauce

(Illustrated on back cover and pages 20/21)

Serves 6

1 fresh coconut	1 onion, chopped
2$\frac{1}{2}$ cups hot water	1 tablespoon chopped fresh
2 tablespoons ghee	coriander leaves
1 teaspoon cumin seeds	$\frac{1}{2}$-in piece fresh root ginger, grated
6 green chilies	$\frac{1}{2}$ teaspoon sugar
a few curry leaves	salt to taste

1 Pierce two of the eyes in the top of the coconut and drain off the coconut water. Break the nut in half with a hammer, remove and grate the flesh.

2 Reserve 2 tablespoons of the grated coconut. Add the hot water to the remaining coconut and allow to stand for a little while. Chop in a blender and strain through a sieve to obtain coconut milk.

3 Melt the ghee in a saucepan, add the cumin seeds and fry for $\frac{1}{2}$ minute. Slit one of the chilies open and add it to the cumin with the curry leaves. Continue to fry for a few minutes.

4 Grind the reserved coconut, onion, remaining chilies, chopped coriander and ginger to a paste, then add the paste to the pan and continue to fry for a further 1 minute.

5 Stir in the coconut milk, sugar and salt. Bring to the boil, simmer for 10 minutes and serve hot with the Vegetable Ring (page 31).

Zesty Dip

(Illustrated on pages 92/93)

Serves 4

$\frac{2}{3}$ cup thick yogurt	1 cucumber, grated
salt to taste	3 tablespoons light cream
4 large radishes, grated	2 green chilies, chopped

1 Line a bowl with a piece of muslin. Pour in the yogurt and tie the muslin around it. Hang the yogurt over a bowl for 1 hour.

2 Sprinkle salt over the grated radish and cucumber in a colander and leave to stand over a bowl for 30 minutes. Squeeze out the water and dry the vegetables on absorbent paper.

3 Mix the yogurt, cream, chilies, radish, cucumber and salt to taste, then chill thoroughly before serving.

4 Serve as a dip with warm crackers or poppadums (page 77). Alternatively serve as a side dish with curries.

Fruit and Vegetable Raita

(Illustrated on pages 56/57)

Serves 6

1¼ cups thick yogurt
2 tablespoons heavy cream
1 cup grapes
2 cups chopped cabbage
1 banana, sliced

2 dessert apples, chopped
1 cucumber, chopped
2 green chilies, chopped
2 teaspoons cumin seeds
2 teaspoons sugar

1 Lightly whisk the yogurt with the cream. Halve the grapes and remove their seeds, then mix them with the remaining ingredients.

2 Stir these ingredients into the whisked yogurt and pour into a bowl. Chill lightly before serving.

Palak Raita

Serves 6

1 lb fresh spinach leaves or
8-oz packet frozen spinach
2 green chilies, chopped
2 pinches pepper

2 pinches sugar
1 teaspoon salt
2 cups yogurt
a little chili powder

1 Cook the fresh spinach in boiling water, then drain thoroughly and finely chop it. Cook the frozen spinach, if used, according to the instructions on the packet and drain thoroughly.

2 Stir the spinach, chilies, pepper, sugar and salt into the yogurt and chill thoroughly before serving sprinkled with a little chili powder.

Spicy Yogurt

(Illustrated on page 100)

Serves 6

3 tablespoons chopped fresh mint
leaves
1 tablespoon water
2 cups yogurt
1 tablespoon finely chopped fresh
coriander leaves

1 teaspoon sugar
1 teaspoon salt
1 teaspoon cumin seeds
chili powder (optional)

1 Grind or purée the mint with the water, then beat into the yogurt and add the coriander, sugar and salt.

2 Lightly roast the cumin seeds in a heavy-based skillet, then grind them to a powder and add to the yogurt mixture. Stir well to make sure all the ingredients are combined.

3 Chill the mixture thoroughly. If you like, sprinkle a little chili powder over before the spicy yogurt is served.

Green Chutney

1 bunch fresh coriander leaves
4 green chilies
4 tablespoons grated fresh coconut

1 teaspoon salt
3 teaspoons sugar
1½ teaspoons lemon juice

1 Trim most of the stalks off the coriander and place the leaves in a blender.

2 Add the remaining ingredients and blend them together to form a paste, adding a little water if necessary. Use either as an accompaniment or as required in the recipes.

Note: Fresh chutney does not store very well but it can be kept in a covered container in the refrigerator for a few days.

Poppadums

(Illustrated on pages 52/53 and 85)

There are numerous varieties of poppadums available, sold in packets ready for cooking. You can either roast poppadums directly over a gas flame or under a hot broiler. Alternatively they can be deep or shallow fried in oil until crisp.

If you like, before serving the cooked poppadums, sprinkle a little chili powder or fresh coriander and grated coconut over them.

Gado Gado

(Illustrated on page 29)

Serves 8–10

$\frac{2}{3}$ cup long-grain rice
$1\frac{1}{2}$ cups water
salt to taste
10 green beans, diagonally sliced
3 carrots, coarsely grated
2 cups bean sprouts
2 cups cabbage, shredded
1 cucumber, cut into matchstick strips
2 tomatoes, thinly sliced
2 teaspoons sugar
$1\frac{1}{2}$ teaspoons salt
a little pepper

DRESSING
2 tablespoons oil
1 onion, chopped
$\frac{1}{2}$ cup salted peanuts
1 tablespoon chopped tamarind
1 tablespoon molasses
$1-1\frac{1}{2}$ teaspoons chili powder
$1\frac{1}{4}$ cups water
salt to taste
3 tablespoons light cream
GARNISH
2 onions, sliced and fried
a few cooked poppadums (page 77), crushed
a little chili powder or fried chopped chilies

1 Place the rice in a saucepan with the water and a generous pinch of salt. Bring to the boil, cover the pan and reduce the heat. Cook gently for about 15–20 minutes or until all the water has been absorbed. Allow to cool.

2 Lightly cook the green beans in boiling salted water. Drain the beans and place them in a large bowl.

3 Mix the carrots, bean sprouts, cabbage, cucumber and tomatoes with the beans. Season with the sugar, salt and pepper, mix well and chill.

4 To make the dressing, heat the oil in a saucepan, add the chopped onion and cook until soft. Allow to cool.

5 Grind the peanuts, tamarind, molasses, chili powder and onion together to make a paste. Gradually blend in the water, salt and cream.

6 Arrange the vegetable mixture on a large serving dish and top with the rice.

7 Pour the dressing over the rice. Top with the fried onions, poppadums and a little chili powder or fried chilies. Serve immediately.

Breads

Breads play an important part in the Indian menu, for they are used as an implement to scoop up the food from the plate and mop up the rich sauces. Several types of bread are included in this chapter. In preparation, the dough can be kneaded and rolled several times, with or without a raising agent, then shaped into rounds, ovals or triangular pancakes. Some breads are deep-fried in ghee, others are dry fried on a tava or griddle and certain varieties are baked. Whatever the cooking method the end result should be light and browned, often puffed or crisp, and the bread should always be served freshly cooked.

Spicy vegetable stuffings are added in some recipes to give satisfying moist breads which are absolutely delicious. And there is also a recipe for a sweet bread – Nariyal ni Mithi Rotli. This is served with savory dishes and the result is quite mouth watering.

Parathas

Makes 10–12

4 cups whole-grain flour
½ teaspoon salt
¼ cup ghee

1½ cups water
about ¼ cup ghee, melted to
brush over the dough

1 Sift the flour into a bowl with the salt. Rub in the ghee, then gradually mix in the water to make a soft dough.

2 Divide the dough into 10–12 equal portions and shape each into a ball. Roll each ball of dough into a circle measuring about 5–6 in. in diameter.

3 Brush each round with melted ghee and fold in half. Brush with more melted ghee and fold into quarters. Roll out the folded dough once more, into rounds similar in size to the original circles.

4 Cook one round at a time on a hot griddle or heavy-based skillet, turning once. After 1 minute brush a little extra ghee around the edges – they should puff up.

5 Turn the paratha and fry the other side. The bread is ready when browned on both sides.

Chapatis

(Illustrated on page 17)

Makes 8–10

2 cups whole-grain flour   2 teaspoons oil or ghee   about ⅔ cup water

1 Sift the flour into a bowl, add the oil or ghee and gradually mix in the water to make a soft dough. Knead the dough for a few minutes, then set it aside in a covered bowl for 30 minutes.

2 Break off small pieces of the dough and roll them out on a floured surface to make thin circles.

3 Cook the chapatis on a hot griddle or heavy-based skillet for a few seconds on one side. Turn and cook the other side for a few seconds.

4 Holding the chapati with tongs, finish cooking it directly over a gas flame until it puffs up like a ball. Alternatively place the bread under a hot broiler.

5 Flatten, spread with a little ghee and serve hot.

Paneer Mutter Korma (page 44) and Saffron Pullao (page 67)

Potato Roti

(Illustrated on page 104/105)

Makes 4

3 large potatoes, boiled and mashed
2 tablespoons chopped fresh
coriander leaves
3 green chilies, chopped

2 tablespoons butter, melted
1 teaspoon salt
about 1 cup all-purpose flour
ghee for frying

1 Mix all the ingredients thoroughly, adding enough flour to make a soft dough. Water is not required for this purpose.

2 Divide the dough into four equal portions, then roll each on a floured surface to give a round measuring about 6 in. in diameter.

3 Heat a griddle or heavy-based skillet. Cook the roti dry on the hot surface, or first grease the pan with a little ghee.

4 When the underside is browned, turn the roti over and cook on the second side. Serve immediately with curry or dal.

5 Alternatively, the roti can be deep fried in hot ghee.

Sabji Parathas

Makes 8

2 cups all-purpose flour
$\frac{1}{2}$ teaspoon salt
2 teaspoons melted butter
$\frac{2}{3}$ cup milk
STUFFING
2 tablespoons ghee
1 onion, finely chopped
$1\frac{1}{2}$ cups cooked vegetables – for
example, green beans, carrots and
peas

1 small potato, boiled and finely
chopped
salt to taste
2 green chilies, chopped
$\frac{1}{2}$ teaspoon chili powder
2 pinches garam masala (page 124)
2 tablespoons chopped fresh
coriander leaves
ghee for cooking

1 Sift the flour and salt into a bowl. Mix the butter and milk to make a soft dough, adding a little extra milk if necessary. Knead the dough thoroughly on a lightly floured surface.

2 To make the stuffing, melt the ghee in a skillet. Add the onion and cook until soft.

3 Finely chop the cooked vegetables and add to the skillet with the potato, salt, chilies, chili powder, garam masala and chopped coriander. Cook for 1 minute, then cool the mixture.

4 Divide the dough into eight equal portions and roll out very thinly into 6-in circles.

5 Put 2 tablespoons of stuffing in the centre of each paratha. Fold in half to make a semi-circle, pressing the edges together to keep the filling in.

6 Heat a griddle or heavy-based skillet and cook the parathas on one side only. Fold into quarters, turning the cooked side inside.

7 Spread more ghee on top, turn over and cook, turning once, until browned on both sides. Serve immediately.

Khamiri Pea Puris

(Illustrated on pages 24/25)

Makes 8

1½ cups all-purpose flour	1 teaspoon cumin seeds
1½ cups whole-grain flour	2 tablespoons chopped fresh
½ cake compressed yeast	coriander leaves
or 1 teaspoon dry yeast	6–7 green chilies, chopped
1 teaspoon sugar	4 teaspoons mango powder
1 cup lukewarm water	1½ cups peas, cooked and mashed
2 tablespoons melted ghee	ghee for cooking
1 teaspoon salt	

1 Mix the flours in a bowl and make a well in the centre.

2 Cream the compressed yeast with the sugar. Pour in half the water and allow to stand for about 5 minutes or until foamy. If using dry yeast, sprinkle it over the water and sugar in a jug and allow to stand for 5–10 minutes until dissolved and foamy. Pour into the well in the flour.

3 Add half the ghee, salt and remaining water. Gradually stir the flour into the yeast liquid to make a soft dough.

4 Knead the dough thoroughly until smooth and elastic.

5 Place the dough in a floured bowl and cover with a damp cloth. Leave to stand in a warm place for 30 minutes.

6 Meanwhile, prepare the stuffing. Heat the remaining ghee in a skillet and fry the cumin seeds in it for 1 minute. Add all the remaining ingredients, season to taste and mix well. Set aside to cool.

7 Divide the dough into eight equal portions. Roll out each to give a 4-in circle. Place a little of the filling in the middle of the rolled out dough and fold the edges up to enclose the pea mixture completely.

8 Flatten the stuffed dough and roll out to give a 4-in round. Repeat with the remaining dough and stuffing. Leave the prepared puris to stand on a floured board for 10–15 minutes.

9 Melt enough ghee to give a 1-in depth of fat in a deep fryer or saucepan.

10 Fry the puris one at a time until golden brown, turning once to brown both sides. Drain on absorbent paper and serve immediately.

Vegetable-stuffed Puris

Makes 10

2 slices bread	MASALA WATER
3 cups all-purpose flour	2 teaspoons mango powder
$\frac{1}{2}$ teaspoon salt	1 teaspoon chili powder
1 tablespoon melted ghee	$\frac{1}{2}$ teaspoon garam masala (page 124)
$1\frac{1}{2}$ cups water	$\frac{1}{4}$ teaspoon salt
ghee for deep frying	$\frac{2}{3}$ cup water
6–7 potatoes, boiled and mashed	ONION MASALA
$\frac{3}{4}$ cup peas, cooked and mashed	1 teaspoon chili powder
3 green chilies, chopped	1 teaspoon mango powder
2 teaspoons garam masala (page 124)	$\frac{1}{2}$ teaspoon salt
1 teaspoon lemon juice	1 large onion, finely chopped
salt to taste	ghee for cooking
about $\frac{2}{3}$ cup dry breadcrumbs	Chilies in vinegar (page 16) to serve
oil for deep frying	

1 Cut the crusts off the bread and soak the slices in water for a few minutes. Squeeze out the water and crumble the bread into a bowl.

2 Sift three-quarters of the flour and the $\frac{1}{2}$ teaspoon salt over the bread. Add the ghee and $\frac{2}{3}$ cup water, then mix and knead to make a dough.

3 Divide the dough into ten equal portions and roll into thick puris measuring about 6 in. in diameter.

4 Heat the ghee for deep frying to 350 F, then fry the puris very lightly until puffed but not browned. Drain and set aside.

5 Mix the potatoes, peas, chilies, garam masala, lemon juice and salt to taste. Shape into long rolls about the size of frankfurters or sausages.

6 Make a batter by mixing the remaining flour and water with salt to taste. Dip the potato rolls in batter, then roll in the breadcrumbs.

7 Heat the oil for deep frying to 350 F, add the potato rolls and cook until golden brown. Drain on absorbent paper and keep hot.

8 To make the masala water, mix the mango and chili powders, garam masala, salt and water.

9 Mix all the ingredients for the onion masala and set aside.

10 Heat a small, heavy-based skillet and grease it lightly with ghee. Cook the puris again for a few minutes on each side until puffed and golden brown.

11 Brush a little masala water over each puri, sprinkle with a little of the onion masala and a few chilies in vinegar. Put a potato roll in the centre, fold the puris over and serve immediately.

Rajma Curry (page 51), Banana Nut Salad (page 74) and Poppadums (page 77)

Parathas Stuffed with Vegetables and Cheese

Makes 5–6

3 carrots
1 small cauliflower
2 potatoes
5 green chilies, chopped
4 tablespoons chopped fresh
coriander leaves
1-in piece fresh root ginger, grated
$\frac{1}{4}$ cup ghee
1 teaspoon cumin seeds

1 cup peas
$1\frac{1}{2}$ cups water
4 tablespoons grated hard cheese
salt to taste
$1\frac{1}{2}$ cups all-purpose flour
$1\frac{1}{2}$ cups whole-grain flour
$\frac{3}{4}$ teaspoon salt
ghee for cooking

1 Finely chop the carrots, cauliflower and potatoes.

2 Grind 3 chilies, 2 tablespoons of the chopped coriander and the grated ginger to make a paste.

3 Melt half the ghee in a saucepan, add the cumin seeds and fry for about 1 minute. Add the chopped vegetables, peas, paste and 6 tablespoons of the water. Bring to the boil, then cook gently until the vegetables become soft.

4 Roughly mash the vegetables, add the cheese, reserved chopped chilies, chopped coriander and salt. Mix well.

5 Mix the flours with the $\frac{3}{4}$ teaspoon salt and rub in the remaining ghee. Add enough of the remaining water to make a soft dough. Knead well, then divide into 10–12 portions.

6 Roll out the pieces of dough to give 6-in circles. Place one dough circle on a heated, greased griddle or heavy-based skillet, spread a little filling on top and cover with a second circle of dough, pressing the edges together well.

7 Spread a little ghee on top, turn the paratha over and spread more ghee on top. Cook until browned on the underside, then turn and cook until browned on the second side. Serve immediately.

Khamiri Parathas

Makes 5

1½ cups all-purpose flour
1½ cups whole-grain flour
1 teaspoon baking powder
⅔ cup yogurt
1 teaspoon sugar
1 teaspoon salt
1 tablespoon melted ghee
⅔ cup water

STUFFING
salt
1½ cups cabbage, finely shredded
1 cup cauliflower, grated
1 tablespoon chopped fresh
coriander leaves
3–4 green chilies, chopped
½ teaspoon finely chopped fresh root
ginger
ghee for cooking

1 Mix the flours in a bowl and make a well in the centre. Add the baking powder. Pour in the yogurt and leave to stand for 1 minute. Add the sugar, salt, ghee and water. Mix the ingredients to make a soft dough.

2 Knead the dough until smooth and set aside in a covered bowl for 3–4 hours.

3 Meanwhile, prepare the stuffing. Sprinkle salt over the shredded cabbage and grated cauliflower, then leave to stand for a few minutes. Squeeze out all the water and place the vegetables in a bowl. Add the chopped coriander, chilies, ginger and salt to taste. Mix well.

4 Divide the dough into ten equal portions and roll out each to give a 4-in circle. Spread a little filling on one circle of dough, cover with a second circle and press together well. Roll out into a paratha measuring about 8 in. in diameter. Repeat with the rest of the dough and stuffing.

5 Heat a griddle or heavy-based skillet. Grease the pan with a little ghee. Cook the parathas, one at a time, until browned on the underside.

6 Spread a little ghee on the top of the paratha, then turn it over and cook until browned on the second side. Serve immediately.

Overleaf *From the left: Paneer Palak Parathas (page 90), Yogurt Kofta Curry (page 47) and Stuffed Potato and Paneer Pears (page 111) with yogurt, chopped tomatoes and grated carrot*

Paneer Palak Parathas

(Illustrated on pages 88/89)

Makes 6

8-oz packet frozen chopped
spinach, thawed
4 tablespoons water
$\frac{1}{2}$ teaspoon lemon juice
$1\frac{1}{2}$ cups all-purpose flour
$1\frac{1}{2}$ cups whole-grain flour
2 tablespoons ghee
1 teaspoon salt
STUFFING
1 cup cauliflower, grated

$\frac{1}{4}$ cup paneer (page 122),
crumbled
1 tablespoon chopped fresh
coriander leaves
3 green chilies, chopped
$\frac{1}{2}$ teaspoon finely chopped fresh root
ginger
salt to taste
ghee for cooking
yogurt to serve

1 Mix the spinach with 2 tablespoons of the water and lemon juice in a blender.

2 Mix both the flours in a bowl and rub in the ghee. Add the salt.

3 Stir in the blended spinach and enough of the remaining water to make a soft dough.

4 Mix all the ingredients for the stuffing.

5 Divide the dough into six. Roll out each portion of the dough into a circle measuring about 6 in. in diameter.

6 Put about 2–3 tablespoons of the stuffing in the centre and fold the edges up over the filling, pressing them together to seal in the mixture.

7 Roll out again to make a thick, 6 in circle. Repeat with the rest of the dough and filling.

8 Heat a griddle or heavy-based skillet and grease it generously with ghee. Cook the parathas on one side, spread ghee on top, then turn over and cook on the second side. Serve immediately with yogurt.

Koki

Makes 6–8

2 cups whole-grain flour
$\frac{3}{4}$ teaspoon salt
2 onions, chopped
2 tablespoons chopped fresh
coriander leaves
2–3 green chilies, chopped

1 teaspoon cumin seeds
1 teaspoon grated fresh root ginger
2 tablespoons melted ghee
about $\frac{2}{3}$ cup water
ghee for cooking

1 Sift the flour and salt into a bowl. Add all the remaining ingredients, mixing in the water to make a stiff dough.

2 Knead the dough lightly, then divide it into six or eight equal portions. Roll out each portion into a circle measuring about 6 in. in diameter. Using a sharp knife make a few light, horizontal slits on one side of each koki.

3 Grease a griddle or heavy-based skillet with ghee and cook the breads, turning once, until browned on both sides. Serve hot.

Indian Teacakes

(Illustrated on page 100)

Makes 6

2 cups plus 2 tablespoons all-purpose
flour
$\frac{3}{4}$ teaspoon salt
$\frac{1}{2}$ cake compressed yeast
$\frac{3}{4}$ teaspoon sugar
$\frac{3}{4}$ cup plus 2 tablespoons
warm water
2 teaspoons melted ghee
2 tablespoons ghee
1 onion, chopped

2 cups cooked mixed vegetables,
chopped
1 potato, boiled and chopped
2–3 green chilies, chopped
1 teaspoon chili powder
$\frac{1}{2}$ teaspoon garam masala (page 124)
2 tablespoons chopped fresh
coriander leaves
melted ghee or butter to serve

1 Sift the flour and salt into a bowl and make a well in the centre. Cream the yeast and sugar with a little of the warm water, then add the remaining water. Leave to stand for about 10 minutes or until the yeast liquid is foamy.

2 Pour the liquid into the bowl then mix in the flour and add the melted ghee to make a soft dough. Knead the dough for 5 minutes.

3 Place the dough in a greased bowl and cover with a damp cloth. Allow to rise for 25 minutes or until doubled in size.

4 Meanwhile, melt the 2 tablespoons ghee in a saucepan and fry the onion in it for 1 minute.

5 Add the vegetables, chilies, chili powder, garam masala and chopped coriander. Cook for 1 minute, then remove from the heat and allow to cool.

6 Quickly knead the risen dough and divide into six portions. Roll each portion into a 4-in round. Divide the filling between the dough circles and fold the edges up around it.

7 Seal the edges of the dough, then flatten the breads into 6-in rounds.

8 Leave to rise in a warm place for 20–25 minutes, then bake in a hot oven (450F) for 10 minutes and serve hot, brushed with ghee or butter.

Overleaf *From the left: Poppadums (page 77), Three-in-one Rice (page 62), Zesty Dip (page 75) and Bread Koftas in Pumpkin Curry (page 43)*

Methi Roti

Makes 6–8

2 cups whole-grain flour
1 teaspoon salt
1 bunch fresh fenugreek leaves,
finely chopped
1 teaspoon cumin seeds

2 tablespoons chopped fresh
coriander leaves
2–3 green chilies, chopped
½ teaspoon chili powder
about ⅔ cup yogurt
ghee or oil for cooking

1 Sift the flour and salt into a bowl. Add the remaining ingredients and, if required, a little additional yogurt or water to make a dough.

2 Knead the dough lightly, then divide it into six or eight portions. Roll out each portion into a circle measuring about 6 in. in diameter.

3 Grease a heavy-based skillet or griddle with ghee or oil and cook the roti, turning once, until browned on both sides. Serve hot.

Nariyal ni Mithi Rotli

Makes about 10

2 teaspoons ghee
1¼ cups fresh coconut, grated
⅓ cup sugar
½ teaspoon ground cardamom
½ teaspoon grated nutmeg

DOUGH
3 cups whole-grain flour
pinch of salt
1 tablespoon melted ghee
about 1 cup water
ghee for cooking

1 Melt the ghee in a small skillet. Add the coconut and cook gently, stirring continuously until it is lightly colored and totally dry. This takes 15–20 minutes. Set aside to cool.

2 Stir the sugar, ground cardamom and nutmeg into the coconut. Taste and add extra sugar and nutmeg as desired.

3 Sift the flour and salt for the dough into a bowl. Make a well in the centre, then add the ghee and enough water to make a fairly soft dough. Allow to stand, covered, for 30 minutes.

4 Divide the dough into about 20 portions, then roll out each into small circles measuring about 4 in. in diameter. Keep the un-rolled dough covered with a damp cloth.

5 Spread about 1 tablespoon of the filling on each of half the circles of dough and dampen the edges. Press the remaining circles of dough on top, sealing the edges to enclose the filling completely.

6 Grease a griddle or heavy-based skillet and cook the breads, turning once until browned on both sides. Serve with Green Peas Ambti (page 36).

Snacks

Here is a selection of imaginative recipes using vegetables, dals and rice. As well as being ideal for light meals, many of these dishes can be served as accompaniments for the main meal.

Neat patties, savory cakes and balls cooked in a very light batter or breadcrumbs form the majority of recipes in this chapter. They are easily eaten with the fingers, deliciously spiced and offer an excellent contrast in food textures.

If you would like to serve a separate first course to open the meal, then many of the recipes in this chapter would make tasty starters – Vegetable Rolls, for example, are interesting pancakes filled with a chutney, salad and a deep-fried vegetable mixture.

Whenever you want a snack to eat between meals, or if you feel in doubt as to how best to complete your menu, try one or two of these well-flavored, interesting and quite satisfying savories.

Semolina Pancakes

(Illustrated on page 64)

Makes about 18

2 cups semolina
¾ cup yogurt
1 cup water
1 cup frozen corn, cooked
1 tablespoon chopped fresh
coriander leaves

4–5 green chilies, chopped
½ teaspoon baking soda
2 teaspoons ghee or oil
2 pinches asafoetida
salt to taste
ghee or oil for cooking

1 Mix the semolina, yogurt and water together in a bowl and allow to stand for at least 5–6 hours.

2 Add all the remaining ingredients and mix together thoroughly to form a batter.

3 Melt the ghee or heat the oil in a greaseless skillet. Drop spoonfuls of the batter into the skillet and cook until browned on one side, turn over and cook the second side. Serve hot.

Note: When the pancakes are cooked on one side, they can be sprinkled with finely chopped carrots and chopped fresh coriander leaves. Turn over and cook the second side.

Bread Snack

Serves 4

2 tablespoons oil
2 teaspoons mustard seeds
10–12 slices bread, made into
crumbs
2 onions, chopped
2 curry leaves
2 tomatoes, chopped
4–5 green chilies, chopped

1 teaspoon finely chopped fresh root
ginger
1 tablespoon tomato purée
juice of 1 lemon
2 tablespoons chopped fresh
coriander leaves
salt to taste

1 Heat the oil in a skillet and fry the mustard seeds for ½ minute. Add the breadcrumbs, onions and curry leaves, then continue to fry until the onions are lightly browned.

2 Add the tomatoes, chilies and ginger. Fry for 1 minute. Stir in the tomato purée, lemon juice, coriander and salt to taste. Cook stirring for 2–3 minutes.

3 Serve immediately, in small portions as a snack or accompaniment with vegetable curries.

Tomato Medley

Serves 2

4 tomatoes
1 large potato
2 tablespoons butter
2 cloves garlic, pressed
1 onion, chopped
pinch of ajwain seeds

$\frac{1}{2}$ teaspoon chili powder
2 teaspoons sugar
salt to taste
3 tablespoons grated hard cheese
$\frac{1}{2}$ cup button mushrooms,
chopped

1 Place the tomatoes in a bowl and pour in enough boiling water to cover them. Allow to stand for 1 minute, then drain, skin and chop the tomatoes.

2 Cut the potato into small cubes.

3 Melt the butter and fry the garlic and onion in it for 1 minute. Stir in the tomatoes, potato, ajwain seeds, chili powder, sugar and salt. Cook for a few minutes until the potato cubes are soft.

4 Stir in the grated cheese and chopped mushrooms and serve immediately.

Mee Goreng

Serves 4

$\frac{1}{2}$ lb egg noodles
5 large onions
5 cloves garlic
6 dried red chilies
$\frac{1}{2}$-in piece fresh root ginger, grated
6 tablespoons oil
4 tomatoes, chopped

2 cups bean sprouts
4 cups cabbage, shredded
3–4 tablespoons tomato catsup
(optional)
salt to taste
$\frac{1}{2}$ cucumber, sliced

1 Cook the noodles in plenty of boiling salted water, drain and set aside.

2 Chop two of the onions and grind them to a paste with the garlic, chilies and ginger. Slice the remaining onions.

3 Heat the oil and fry the sliced onions until they are lightly browned. Add the paste and fry for a further 2–3 minutes. Add the tomatoes and cook for 1 minute.

4 Stir in the bean sprouts and cabbage, then continue to cook for 2 minutes. Add the noodles, tomato catsup (if used) and salt. Mix well. Cook for a few minutes until heated through, then serve hot with the sliced cucumber.

Vegetarian Kababs

Serves 4

1 small pumpkin or marrow, peeled and grated	5 green chilies, chopped
2 onions, grated	1 teaspoon black cumin seeds
2 medium potatoes, grated	oil for deep frying
salt	MASALA
4 tablespoons gram flour	1 teaspoon chili powder
2 tablespoons chopped fresh coriander leaves	1 teaspoon mango powder
	$\frac{1}{2}$ teaspoon salt
	2 onions, chopped

1 Place the grated pumpkin or marrow, onions and potatoes in a colander. Sprinkle 2 teaspoons of salt over them and leave to stand for 20 minutes. Squeeze all the water out of the vegetables and place them in a bowl.

2 Add salt to taste, the gram flour, coriander leaves, chilies and black cumin seeds. Shape the mixture into small balls about the size of walnuts. Meanwhile, heat the oil for deep frying to 350 F, then fry the balls a few at a time until golden.

3 Drain the kababs on absorbent paper and, while they are still hot, flatten them with a spatula to form little cakes.

4 Mix all the ingredients for the masala.

5 To serve, deep fry the kababs to reheat them and sprinkle with the masala.

Vegetable Croquettes

Makes 24

1 cup plus 4 tablespoons all-purpose flour	2 onions, finely chopped
salt to taste	$\frac{1}{2}$ teaspoon turmeric
$1\frac{1}{4}$ cups water	2 pinches baking soda
2 medium potatoes	1 tablespoon chopped fresh coriander leaves
2 carrots	4–5 green chilies, chopped
$\frac{1}{2}$ lb green beans	about 1 cup vermicelli, broken into small pieces
1 lb cabbage	ghee for deep frying
2 tablespoons ghee	

1 Make a batter by mixing the 1 cup of flour and a pinch of salt with the water. Beat thoroughly until smooth and set aside.

2 Chop the potatoes, carrots, green beans and cabbage very finely.

3 Melt the ghee in a saucepan and fry the onions in it for a few minutes. Add the prepared vegetables, turmeric, baking soda and salt to taste. Cover and cook gently until soft – about 30 minutes.

4 Sprinkle the 4 tablespoons flour over the vegetables and cook for 2 minutes. Remove the pan from the heat. Add the chopped coriander and chilies and mix well. Allow the mixture to cool, lightly flour your hands and shape the mixture into croquettes.

5 Lightly beat the batter. Dip the croquettes in the batter, then roll in the broken vermicelli.

6 Heat the ghee for deep frying to 350 F and cook the croquettes until golden brown. Drain on absorbent paper and serve immediately.

Sabzi Wadas

Makes 15

2 onions, chopped
3–4 green chilies
1-in piece of fresh root ginger, grated
2 tablespoons ghee
1 tomato, chopped
1 teaspoon chili powder (optional)
2 tablespoons chopped fresh coriander leaves
a few mint leaves, chopped
4 cups mixed vegetables – for example green beans, eggplant and carrots – cooked and finely chopped

3 large potatoes, boiled and coarsely mashed
salt to taste
$\frac{1}{2}$ cup all-purpose flour
$\frac{2}{3}$ cup water
about $\frac{2}{3}$ cup dry breadcrumbs
oil for deep frying
chili sauce to serve (optional)

1 Grind half the chopped onion with the chilies and ginger to make a paste.

2 Melt the ghee in a saucepan, add the remaining onion and fry for a few minutes. Add the paste and continue to cook for 2 minutes. Add the tomato, chili powder (if used), chopped coriander and mint. Cook for 2 minutes.

3 Stir in the vegetables, mashed potatoes and salt to taste. Mix thoroughly, then allow to cool.

4 Mix the flour and water to make a batter and beat well until smooth.

5 Shape spoonfuls of the vegetable mixture into balls about the size of a small egg. Dip the vegetable balls first in the batter, then roll them lightly in the breadcrumbs.

6 Heat the oil for deep frying to 350 F and fry the balls until golden. Serve hot with chili sauce (if liked).

Vegetable Rolls

(Illustrated on pages 24/25)

Makes 6

4–5 medium potatoes, boiled and
coarsely mashed
2 tablespoons chopped fresh
coriander leaves
3–4 green chilies, chopped
2 teaspoons lemon juice
1 teaspoon garam masala (page 124)
salt to taste
$\frac{1}{2}$ cup gram flour
$1\frac{1}{2}$ cups all-purpose flour
$1\frac{1}{4}$ cups water
chili powder to taste
1 teaspoon baking powder
$1\frac{1}{4}$ cups milk

ghee for frying
oil for deep frying
CHUTNEY
large bunch of fresh coriander
leaves, trimmed
3–4 green chilies, chopped
$\frac{3}{4}$ teaspoon sugar
$\frac{1}{2}$ teaspoon salt
3 tablespoons grated fresh coconut
juice of $\frac{1}{2}$ lemon
SALAD
1 small lettuce, shredded
1 small onion, chopped
2 carrots, grated

1 Mix the potatoes, chopped coriander, chilies, lemon juice, garam masala, and salt to taste. Shape into rolls about 1 in. in diameter and 3–4 in. in length.

2 Mix the gram flour with $\frac{1}{2}$ cup of the all-purpose flour and beat in the water to make a batter. Add salt and chili powder to taste.

3 Mix the remaining all-purpose flour with the baking powder and a pinch of salt. Beat in the milk to make a smooth batter.

4 Melt a little ghee in a greaseless skillet. Pour in a little of the milk batter to make fairly thick pancakes measuring about 6 in. in diameter. Cook until browned underneath, then turn over and cook the second side. Continue until all the batter is used. Layer the pancakes with parchment paper to prevent them sticking. Keep hot.

5 To make the chutney grind the coriander with the chilies, sugar, salt, coconut and lemon juice to form a paste.

6 Heat the oil for deep frying to 350 F. Dip the potato rolls in the prepared water batter and deep fry until golden.

7 Mix the salad ingredients.

8 Spread a little chutney over each pancake. Top with a little of the salad and a potato roll. Fold over and serve.

Masala Dal (page 50), Indian Teacakes (page 91) and Spicy Yogurt (page 77)

Green Peas Renedy

(Illustrated on back cover and pages 56/57)

Makes 6

4 cups peas	2 pinches baking soda
10 green chilies, chopped	juice of 2 lemons
$\frac{3}{4}$ cup paneer (page 122)	$\frac{1}{2}$ teaspoon sugar
salt to taste	$\frac{3}{4}$ cup all-purpose flour
6 teaspoons oil	$\frac{3}{4}$ cup plus 2 tablespoons water
5 potatoes, boiled and mashed	1 cup dry breadcrumbs
$\frac{1}{4}$ teaspoon turmeric	oil for deep frying

1 Mash the peas with the chilies. Grate the paneer, then mash it with salt to taste. Shape the paneer into six small balls about the size of walnuts.

2 Heat half the oil in a saucepan, add the mashed potatoes, turmeric and salt to taste. Mix well and cool.

3 Heat the remaining oil in another saucepan. Add the peas, baking soda, lemon juice, sugar and salt to taste. Cook for a few minutes. Cool the mixture.

4 Shape spoonfuls of the potato mixture into thin round cakes measuring about 3–4 in. in diameter. Put a paneer ball in each and fold the potato around it to enclose the paneer completely. Knead lightly until smooth. Press a layer of the pea mixture around the potatoes.

5 Mix the flour and water to a smooth batter, beating thoroughly until smooth. Dip the balls in the batter, then roll in the breadcrumbs.

6 Heat the oil for deep frying to 350 F, add the balls and cook until golden brown. Drain on absorbent paper, cut in half and serve immediately.

Corn Pancakes

Makes 15–20

12 ears of fresh corn	3–4 green chilies, chopped
4 tablespoons all-purpose flour	salt to taste
$\frac{1}{4}$ teaspoon baking powder	ghee for cooking
4 tablespoons light cream	TO SERVE
4 tablespoons milk	a little butter
1 teaspoon melted butter	Green Chutney (page 77)
1 tablespoon chopped fresh	
coriander leaves	

1 Strip off and reserve the husks from the corn. Discard the silk. Place the ears in boiling salted water and simmer for 10–15 minutes, or until the corn is tender. Drain and cool slightly.

2 Remove the corn kernels from the ears with a sharp knife or fork and grind coarsely. Add all the other ingredients to the ground corn and mix well.

3 Rinse the reserved husk and dry on absorbent paper. Spread about 1 tablespoon of the mixture on one half of each husk and fold the other half over to enclose the filling.

4 Heat a heavy-based skillet and grease lightly with ghee. Cook the stuffed corn husks on both sides until the filling has set.

5 Dot with butter and serve immediately with the chutney.

Moong Dal Handvo

Serves 4

1½ cups moong dal
2 tablespoons oil
2 onions, chopped
2 carrots, chopped
4 cups cabbage, chopped
¼ teaspoon monosodium glutamate
salt to taste

2 tablespoons yogurt
1 teaspoon baking soda
2 tablespoons chopped fresh
coriander leaves
6–8 green chilies, chopped
juice of ½ lemon
pinch of asafoetida

1 Soak the moong dal for at least 5 hours or overnight. Grind to make a coarse paste.

2 Heat the oil, add the onions, carrots, cabbage, monosodium glutamate and salt to taste. Cook for a few minutes.

3 Stir the yogurt, baking soda, chopped coriander, chilies, lemon juice, asafoetida and salt to taste into the moong dal paste. Add half the cooked vegetables, mix well, then leave to stand for 10–15 minutes.

4 Spread most of the remaining vegetables in the base of a greased ovenproof dish. Spread the moong dal mixture on top. Finally cover with the last of the vegetables. Cover and bake in a hot oven (400F) for 40–45 minutes.

5 Turn out on to a serving dish and serve hot with buttermilk (if liked).

Overleaf *From the left: Potato Roti (page 82), Cucumber Salad (page 74) and Masala Gobhi (page 39)*

Moong Dal Pudas

(Illustrated on page 61)

Makes 24

2 cups moong dal
1 cup buttermilk
3 large tomatoes, finely chopped
1 small cucumber, finely chopped
5 green chilies, finely chopped
3 teaspoons chopped fresh coriander
leaves

$\frac{1}{4}$ teaspoon turmeric
pinch of asafoetida
salt to taste
butter or ghee for cooking

1 Soak the moong dal in cold water to cover for at least 5 hours. Grind coarsely and place in a bowl.

2 Add the buttermilk, tomatoes, cucumber, chilies, coriander, turmeric, asafoetida and salt. Mix well and set aside for 1 hour.

3 Lightly grease a griddle or skillet. Drop large spoonfuls of the mixture into the griddle or skillet and cook until lightly set and browned on the underside. Turn over and cook until browned on the second side. Serve immediately.

Moong Dal Tikkas

Makes 10

1 cup moong dal
4 green chilies
2 cups cabbage, chopped
1 onion, chopped
pinch of asafoetida
1 tablespoon gram flour
$\frac{1}{2}$ teaspoon baking soda

$\frac{1}{2}$ teaspoon lemon juice
1 tablespoon chopped fresh
coriander leaves
salt to taste
butter or ghee for cooking
mango chutney to serve

1 Soak the moong dal overnight in cold water to cover.

2 Next day, grind the dal with the chilies. Add the cabbage, onion, asafoetida, gram flour, baking soda, lemon juice, chopped coriander and salt to taste. Set aside in the refrigerator or a cool place for 1 hour.

3 Form small spoonfuls of the moong dal mixture into balls about the size of a large egg, then flatten them to form small patties.

4 Lightly grease a skillet with butter or ghee and cook the patties a few at a time, turning once, until browned on both sides. Serve hot with mango chutney.

Cabbage Wadas

(Illustrated on pages 52/53)

Makes 8–12

2 cups gram dal
7–8 green chilies
7 cups cabbage, shredded
1 carrot, finely chopped
1 onion, finely chopped

salt to taste
2 tablespoons chopped fresh
coriander leaves
oil for deep frying
Green Chutney (page 77) to serve

1 Soak the gram dal overnight in cold water to cover.

2 Set aside about a quarter of the soaked dal. Grind the remainder with the chilies. Add the cabbage, carrot, onion, salt to taste and chopped coriander to the ground dal along with the remaining gram dal.

3 Take spoonfuls of the mixture and knead into small thick cakes measuring 2 in. in diameter.

4 Heat the oil for deep frying to 350 F, add the cakes, a few at a time, and cook until golden. Drain on absorbent paper and serve immediately with green chutney.

Overleaf *From the left: Paneer and Coconut Balls (page 114), Malai Pudas (page 117) and Bundi Laddoo (page 116)*

Rice and Cheese Balls

Makes about 20

⅓ cup long-grain rice
1¼ cups water
salt to taste
3 tablespoons all-purpose flour
2 green chilies, chopped
2 pinches baking soda

4 tablespoons grated hard cheese
½ teaspoon mustard powder
BATTER
¾ cup plus 2 tablespoons water
½ cup all-purpose flour
ghee or oil for deep frying

1 Place the rice in a saucepan, pour in the water and add a little salt. Bring to the boil, then cover the pan, reduce the heat and cook for 25–30 minutes or until all the water is absorbed. The cooked rice should be sticky.

2 Mix the rice with the flour, chopped chilies, baking soda and salt until the ingredients bind together.

3 Roll small spoonfuls of the mixture into balls about the size of a walnut, then flatten each to form a round shape.

4 Mix the grated cheese with the mustard and place a little in the middle of each rice cake. Carefully fold the edges over the cheese and roll into a neat ball, enclosing the cheese completely in the rice mixture.

5 Gradually beat the water into the flour to make a smooth thin batter. Meanwhile, heat the ghee or oil for deep frying to 350 F. Dip the rice balls in the batter, then fry in the hot ghee or oil until golden brown.

6 Drain on absorbent paper and serve hot.

Stuffed Potato and Paneer Pears

(Illustrated on pages 88/89)

Makes 10

2 tablespoons butter
1 onion, chopped
1½ teaspoons ground cumin
½ cup peas, cooked
1 cup paneer (page 122), chopped
3–4 green chilies, chopped
1 tablespoon chopped fresh coriander leaves
½ teaspoon garam masala (page 124)

½ teaspoon chili powder
salt to taste
1 tablespoon arrowroot
2 cups potatoes, boiled and mashed
¾ cup all-purpose flour
¾ cup plus 2 tablespoons water
oil for deep frying
about ⅔ cup dry breadcrumbs

1 Melt the butter in a skillet, add the onion and cook for 1 minute. Add 1 teaspoon of the ground cumin, the peas, paneer, chilies, chopped coriander, garam masala, chili powder and salt to taste. Remove from the heat and allow to cool.

2 Add the remaining ground cumin, arrowroot and salt to taste to the potatoes and mix thoroughly.

3 Take spoonfuls of the potato mixture (about the size of a small egg) and shape into small round cakes. Mound a little of the pea stuffing in the middle of each. Bring up the edges to enclose the stuffing completely and form a pear-like shape. Chill.

4 Mix the flour and water to make a batter, beating thoroughly until smooth.

5 Heat the oil for deep frying to 350 F. Dip the potato shapes in the batter, roll them in the breadcrumbs, then fry in the hot oil until golden brown. Drain on absorbent paper and serve immediately.

Overleaf *From the top: Malai Pedas (page 114) and Chocolate and Vanilla Barfi (page 115)*

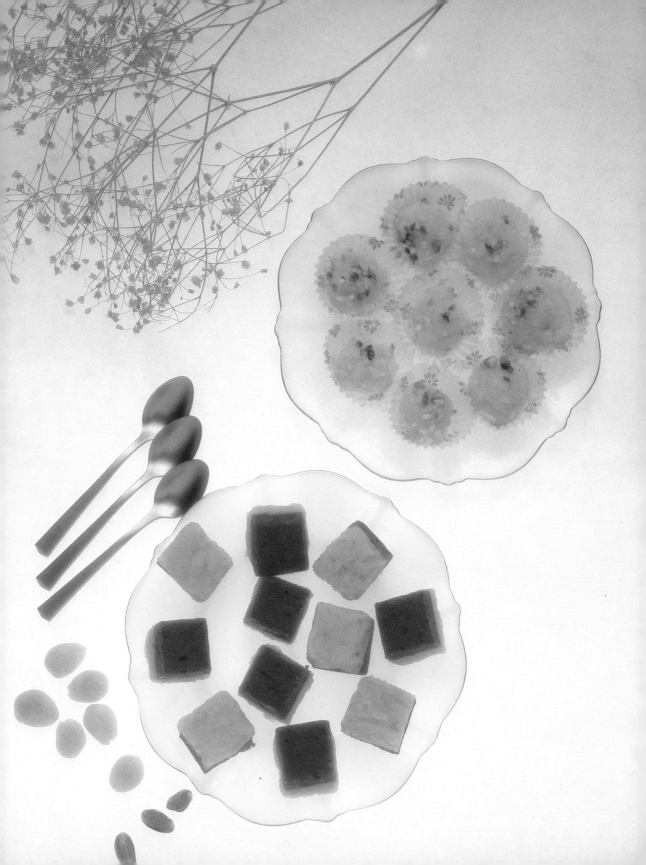

Sweet Dishes

When sweet dishes are served as a part of an Indian meal, they are presented along with the savory food and not as a separate course. However, if you like you can serve any one of these dishes on its own to round off the meal.

Alternatively, why not try serving them as a snack with tea or coffee? The recipes are quite rich in the use of milk and paneer, so they should be served in moderately sized portions. Very fine and expensive edible silver or gold foil is sometimes used to decorate Indian sweetmeats or special dishes, but it is not an essential ingredient. More often, chopped pistachio nuts or almonds are sprinkled over the prepared sweet dish.

Although some of the recipes may need a little extra care in their preparation, particularly for those who are unfamiliar with Indian cooking, the results certainly warrant the effort involved and the dainty candies and desserts will delight your family and guests.

Paneer and Coconut Balls

(Illustrated on pages 108/109)

Makes 30

2½ cups paneer (page 122)
⅔ cup confectioners' sugar
2–3 teaspoons rose water
½ fresh coconut
⅓ cup sugar
¼ teaspoon saffron strands

1 teaspoon milk
edible silver foil for decoration
(optional)
4–5 pistachio nuts, blanched and
chopped

1 Grate the paneer into a bowl, add the confectioners' sugar and rose water. Mix very well to make a dough.

2 Shape spoonfuls of the mixture into small round balls about the size of walnuts.

3 Put the coconut and sugar in a saucepan and cook for 10 minutes over low heat, stirring frequently. Cool.

4 Warm the saffron and milk in a small bowl over a saucepan of hot water. Rub in until the saffron dissolves. Add the saffron milk to the coconut and mix well.

5 Coat the paneer balls with the coconut mixture, rolling them carefully in the palms of your hands.

6 Arrange the paneer and coconut balls on a serving plate and cover with silver foil (if used). Chill thoroughly.

7 To serve, cut each ball into two and decorate with chopped pistachio nuts.

Malai Pedas

(Illustrated on page 112)

Makes 18

4½ cups milk
½ cup sugar
2 pinches citric acid
3 teaspoons water
¼ teaspoon saffron strands
2 tablespoons cornstarch

4–5 green cardamoms, ground
½ cup almonds, blanched and
chopped
10 pistachio nuts, blanched and
chopped

1 Reserve about 4 teaspoons of the milk. Boil the remaining milk in a large heavy-based pan until it is reduced to half its original volume. Add the sugar and continue to boil for 4–5 minutes.

2 Dissolve the citric acid in the water. Add this solution very gradually to the boiling milk until it curdles slightly. This may require anything from half to the entire quantity of acid.

3 Warm the saffron with 1 teaspoon of the reserved milk in a small bowl over a saucepan of hot water. Rub the saffron occasionally until it dissolves, then add to the boiling milk.

4 Blend the cornstarch with the remaining 3 teaspoons of milk until smooth. Stir in a little of the boiling milk, then stir the mixture into the milk in the pan.

5 Go on cooking and stirring until the mixture thickens. Add the ground cardamoms and mix well, then allow to cool. Chill thoroughly for several hours.

6 Using wet hands, shape the cool mixture into balls and put in fluted paper baking cups. Decorate with the almonds and pistachio nuts before serving.

Chocolate and Vanilla Barfi

(Illustrated on page 112)

Makes 18 pieces

1 lb khoya (page 123)	2 teaspoons cocoa
$\frac{2}{3}$ cup sugar	pink food coloring
$\frac{1}{4}$ teaspoon vanilla extract	

1 Mix half the khoya with half the sugar in a saucepan and warm, stirring constantly, over a low heat.

2 After 4–5 minutes, remove a small spoonful of the mixture and test to see if it forms a soft ball when molded between the fingers. When the mixture is ready, remove from the heat and add the vanilla extract. Stir for 1 minute. Spread the mixture into a small cake pan and allow to cool.

3 Cook the remaining khoya and sugar in the same way, but after switching off the heat add the cocoa and a few drops of coloring instead of the vanilla extract. Stir for a little while, then spread evenly over the vanilla mixture. Allow to set for 4–5 hours.

4 Cut into pieces and serve.

Bundi Laddoo

(Illustrated on pages 108/109)

Makes 6–8

1 cup plus 1 tablespoon sugar	ghee for deep frying
1⅔ cups water	1 tablespoon melted ghee
1 tablespoon milk	4 almonds, blanched and sliced
a few saffron strands	4 pistachio nuts, blanched and sliced
1 cup gram flour	4 green cardamoms, crushed
pinch of salt	edible silver foil for decoration
2 pinches baking soda	(optional)

1 Mix the sugar with $\frac{3}{4}$ cup plus 2 tablespoons of the water in a saucepan and put to boil. Add the milk.

2 Boil the sirup steadily until it reaches the soft crack stage: 270–290F on a candy thermometer. At this stage, a few drops of sirup dropped into cold water should form threads which are hard but not brittle.

3 Place the saffron in a small bowl with a little water. Stand the bowl over a saucepan of hot water and rub the saffron occasionally until the strands dissolve.

4 Add the saffron liquid to the sirup, set aside and keep warm.

5 Mix the gram flour, salt and baking soda. Add the remaining water to make a thick batter.

6 Heat the ghee for deep frying to 350F

7 Drop small, even portions of the batter off a spoon into the hot ghee and fry until golden brown. The cooked bundis should be about the size of large peas. Drain on absorbent paper.

8 Put the bundis into the sirup and leave to stand for 10 minutes. Add the melted ghee, almonds, pistachios and cardamoms to the bundis and mix well.

9 Using a wet metal spoon, form the bundis into small balls on a serving platter. Decorate with edible silver foil (if used) and serve.

Malai Pudas

(Illustrated on pages 108/109)

Makes about 20

$\frac{1}{2}$ cup sugar
$\frac{3}{4}$ cup plus 2 tablespoons water
$\frac{1}{2}$ teaspoon saffron strands
a little milk
2 teaspoons rose water (optional)

6 tablespoons light cream
4 tablespoons all-purpose flour
ghee for cooking
shredded blanched almonds and
pistachio nuts to decorate

1 Dissolve the sugar in the water in a saucepan and boil for 5 minutes.

2 Warm the saffron with a little milk in a small bowl over a saucepan of hot water. Rub occasionally until the saffron dissolves, then add to the sirup. Stir in the rose water (if used) and keep the sirup warm.

3 Make a thick batter by gradually beating the cream into the all-purpose flour.

4 Smear very little ghee on a hot griddle or heavy-based skillet and drop small spoonfuls of batter on it to make small pancakes each measuring about 2 in. in diameter. Fry on both sides until golden brown.

5 Dip the pudas in the hot sugar sirup and serve immediately, decorated with almonds and pistachio nuts.

Note: These little pancakes are very similar to griddle cakes. When they are cooked, place the pancakes on a piece of absorbent paper and keep them warm while you use up the remaining batter. The batter can be prepared in advance but make sure that the mixture is not too thick by the time you cook the pancakes. If the batter is too stiff, then add a little extra cream or milk.

Khurmani Ka Mitha

Serves 8

3 cups dried apricots
$\frac{3}{4}$ cup sugar
4 tablespoons dry milk solids
$\frac{1}{2}$ teaspoon ground cardamom
a few drops red food coloring
(optional)

TOPPING
$1\frac{1}{4}$ cups heavy cream
3 tablespoons confectioners' sugar
2 bananas, sliced
2 blanched almonds, sliced
2 pistachio nuts, sliced

1 Soak the apricots in cold water to cover for several hours.

2 Halve and remove the stones if the apricots are whole, then place the drained fruit in a saucepan with the sugar and a little water. Stir over gentle heat until the sugar dissolves, then bring to the boil and simmer for about 15 minutes or until the apricots are cooked.

3 Purée the cooked fruit in a blender or strain it through a sieve, then return the mixture to the saucepan and bring to the boil. Boil, stirring occasionally, for 5 minutes.

4 Stir in the dry milk solids and continue to cook for a few minutes until the mixture thickens slightly. Stir in the ground cardamom and a few drops of food coloring, if liked. Spread this apricot mixture in a greased ovenproof dish or small individual dishes.

5 To make the topping, whip the cream with the confectioners' sugar and spread about half over the apricot base. Arrange the banana slices on top, then spread the remaining cream over.

6 Top with the almonds and pistachio nuts and bake in a moderately hot oven (400F) for 10–15 minutes. Serve immediately.

Orange Sandèsh

Serves 6–8

5 cups milk
juice of 1 lemon
2 oranges
4–5 tablespoons sugar

1 tablespoon orange juice
4 almonds, blanched and sliced
4 pistachio nuts, blanched and sliced

1 Bring the milk to the boil stirring frequently. Add the lemon juice and stir gently, then remove from the heat and stir until the milk curdles. Set aside to cool.

2 Strain the curdled mixture through a sieve lined with muslin cloth. Squeeze out all the liquid, then leave the paneer under a heavy flat weight for at least 1 hour. Meanwhile peel the oranges and remove all the white skin. Cut between the membranes in the oranges and remove the segments.

3 Knead the paneer thoroughly with the sugar, add the orange juice and mix well. Spread half this mixture to form a 5-in square on a plate or dish and arrange half the orange segments on top. Cover with the remaining paneer, spreading it evenly on top.

4 Chill before serving decorated with the remaining orange segments, almonds and pistachio nuts.

Note: The combination of paneer and orange makes this a particularly refreshing sweet – ideal for serving after a hot and spicy main dish. In India, sweet dishes are usually eaten with the main course. If you are planning a traditional Indian meal, follow one of the menus on page 12 and arrange all the food together on the table, then eat small portions at a time from each of the dishes.

Narangi Ni Basundi

Serves 6

5 cups milk
6–7 teaspoons sugar

1 orange
4 tablespoons orange juice

1 Boil the milk and sugar together until it is reduced to one-third of its original quantity. Stir occasionally during cooking to prevent the milk boiling over, then set aside to cool.

2 Peel the orange and remove all the white skin. Cut beween the membranes in the orange and remove the segments. Add these segments with the orange juice to the milk mixture. Mix well and chill for at least 1 hour before serving.

Baked Paneer

Serves 6–8

5 cups milk
juice of 1 lemon
3–4 tablespoons sugar
$\frac{1}{4}$ teaspoon saffron strands

a little milk
$\frac{1}{2}$ teaspoon ground cardamom
$\frac{1}{2}$ teaspoon grated nutmeg
4 almonds, blanched and sliced

1 Bring the milk to the boil, stirring occasionally. Add the lemon juice, remove from the heat and stir gently until the milk curdles and a bluish water floats on top.

2 Strain through a muslin-lined sieve, then hang the paneer in the muslin for at least 2 hours. Knead the paneer thoroughly with the sugar. Soak the saffron in a little warm milk, then rub it in to dissolve the strands.

3 Add the saffron liquid and cardamom to the paneer and mix well. Spread the mixture on a cookie sheet to give a thickness of about $\frac{1}{2}$ in. Sprinkle the nutmeg over and top with the almond slices. Bake in a moderate oven (350F) for 15–20 minutes, then cut into pieces and serve hot or cold.

Basic Recipes

Within this short chapter you will find the key to success for many of the other recipes in the book. Instructions are given for making a vegetable stock and for preparing ghee. Follow the methods for boiling rice and dal to ensure that these staple ingredients are perfectly cooked. And it is well worth roasting and grinding your own spices for freshly prepared garam masala which is far superior to any you can buy ready ground.

Recipes for paneer and khoya are also included. These are two milk-based mixtures which may seem complicated to prepare if you are unfamiliar with Indian cooking; however, the recipes are so clear and simple that when you have prepared them just once you will feel quite confident enough to make them regularly.

Vegetable Stock

3 carrots	2 large tomatoes
$\frac{1}{2}$ lb green beans	small wedge of cabbage
2 large onions	$6\frac{1}{4}$ cups water
2 large potatoes	

1 Roughly chop all the vegetables and place them in a large saucepan with the water. Bring to the boil, cover the pan and simmer steadily for about 2 hours.

2 Cool slightly, then strain through a sieve.

Ghee

1 Melt a quantity of butter (1–4 cups) in a saucepan, then allow it to simmer until a clear yellow liquid is formed and a sediment settles in the base of the pan. This should take about 25 minutes.

2 Carefully strain the clarified butter through muslin, making sure that all the sediment has been removed. Pour into a container with a close-fitting cover.

3 When set, this milky-white or slightly yellow solid can be stored in a covered container for long periods without spoiling.

Paneer

Makes about $\frac{3}{4}$ cup

$4\frac{1}{2}$ cups milk   juice of 1 lemon

1 Bring the milk slowly to the boil. Gradually add the lemon juice while stirring continuously, then continue to stir gently until the milk curdles.

2 Set aside to cool, then strain the curdled milk through a muslin-lined strainer. Squeeze out the liquid (whey), then press the paneer (curds) under a heavy flat weight for at least an hour.

3 Cut into rectangular pieces or use as directed in the recipes.

Khoya

Makes about 1 cup

5 cups milk

1 Bring the milk to the boil in a large heavy-based saucepan. Reduce the heat and simmer the milk, stirring frequently, for about 40–45 minutes.

2 The milk should be reduced to about a quarter of its original volume. When ready, the khoya should resemble a ball of sticky dough. It is used for making Indian candies or as an ingredient in rich vegetable dishes.

Boiled rice

Use long-grain rice for the recipes in this book. Basmati rice gives a better flavor in cooking and old Basmati rice is preferred for a good texture.

For pullaos

$2\frac{1}{2}$ cups long-grain rice   7 cups water

1 Wash the rice thoroughly under running water, then place it in a bowl, cover with water and allow to soak for 30 minutes. Drain.

2 Bring the measured water to the boil, add the rice and bring back to the boil. Reduce the heat and simmer the rice for 15–20 minutes. Take care that it is not overcooked and that the grains remain separate. They should not become mushy.

3 Drain the rice and allow to cool before use.

Note: For everyday use, use a generous 5 cups water and cook the rice as above. Do not drain the rice but cover the pan and cook gently until the rice is cooked and the water has been absorbed.

Boiled Dal

to each 1 cup dal allow 2 cups water

1 Wash the dal under plenty of cold running water.

2 Place the dal in a saucepan with the measured water. Bring to the boil, reduce the heat and cover the pan. Simmer until the water is absorbed and the dal are tender – the cooking time varies depending on the type of dal.

Garam Masala

Makes about 1 tablespoon

3 cinnamon sticks   3 cloves   3 peppercorns

1 Grind the above ingredients together to form a powder. The quantities may be varied to suit individual tastes or for any particular recipe.

2 Generally, for home preparation, garam masala is ground in small quantities for immediate use. Freshly ground masala is usually stronger than the ready made varieties.

Punjabi Garam Masala

Makes about 2 tablespoons

2 cinnamon sticks   1 bay leaf
2 cloves   1 black cardamom
$\frac{1}{2}$ teaspoon cumin seeds   1 green cardamom
generous pinch each of ground
coriander and ground cumin

1 Roast all the spices together in a heavy-based skillet over a gentle heat.

2 Stir the spices continuously until they are lightly colored. They should give off a strong aroma when roasted.

3 Grind all the spices to a powder and store in an airtight container.

Glossary

Ajwain seeds Similar in appearance to celery seeds, with a strong, spicy flavor.

Aniseeds Small, brown and oval in shape, these seeds have a liquorice flavor.

Asafoetida A strong smelling powder with a distinct flavor, it is obtained from the gum of a plant and should be used only in small quantities.

Beans, black Small oval beans with shiny black skins.

Beans, dried broad Dried common broad beans, slightly brown in color with wrinkled skins.

Beans, red kidney Fairly large oval beans with red skins. The beans should be boiled for 3 minutes to destroy natural toxins.

Cardamoms, black Large hairy pods which are black in color. They are not as readily available as the green variety.

Cardamoms, green Pale green pods about the size of small peas, they are used either whole or the small seeds are extracted and ground.

Chick peas Small, creamy-colored and similar in appearance to hazelnuts, these pulses have a nutty flavor. Also known as garbanzos and available canned.

Chilies Either green or red, chilies vary in strength but the seeds are always hot and should be removed if you prefer mild dishes. The following types are usually available:

> **dried red** Small wrinkled hot red chilies.
>
> **green** Fairly small chilies that vary in strength depending on the type. Generally, the long wrinkled chilies are very hot while the small plump ones may be either hot or mild.
>
> **mild red** Small plump Kashmiri chilies that are rounded in shape and not as pungent as the long wrinkled varieties.
>
> **red** Wrinkled, long red chilies or short and slightly plump with a fiery taste.

Cinnamon sticks Curled thin pieces of bark from the cinnamon tree. They are about 4 in long with a strong smell and flavor.

Coriander leaves The fresh leaves look like feathery parsley and are sometimes sold as Chinese parsley. They have a pungent smell and strong flavor.

Coriander seeds These seeds are small, pale and round. They are used either whole or ground.

Cumin seeds White or black, these small long seeds are used either whole or ground.

Curry leaves Small, dark green and shiny, these leaves of neem trees are sold dried and are sometimes available fresh. Fresh curry leaves should be used if available and bay leaves may be substituted.

Dals These are skinned and split pulses.

Fenugreek leaves These are used as a vegetable in Indian cooking or they are sometimes added in small quantities to flavor dishes. They are sometimes available fresh from Indian greengrocers.

Fenugreek seeds Small hard seeds, dull yellow in color and almost rectangular in shape, they are used either whole or ground. They have a bitter taste.

Garam masala This is a mixture of spices ground together (page 124).

Ghee Clarified butter (page 122). Available in cans from specialist shops.

Ginger, fresh root This is a tough, fibrous root with a fairly thick skin. It can be grated on a coarse grater.

Gram flour Either Bengal gram flour or chick pea flour, also known as besan.

Khoya Milk which has been boiled until thick and condensed (page 123).

Mango powder This is a sour powder which is made from dried raw green mangoes.

Masoor dal Skinned and split red lentils.

Moong dal Skinned and split mung beans.

Paneer Indian cream cheese (page 122).

Tamarind The dried pods of the tamarind tree, they are black and sticky with a sour taste. Tamarind paste is also available from specialist shops.

Toovar dal Skinned and split red beans.

Urad dal Skinned and split black beans.

Index

Madhur Jaffrey's cookbook

Madhur Jaffrey's cookbook